Eight sessions for
a children's club

Copyright © Mary Moody 2008
First published 2008
ISBN 978 1 84427 314 0

Scripture Union, 207–209 Queensway, Bletchley, Milton Keynes, MK2 2EB, United Kingdom.
Email: info@scriptureunion.org.uk
Website: www.scriptureunion.org.uk

Scripture Union Australia
Locked Bag 2, Central Coast Business Centre, NSW 2252, Australia
Website: www.scriptureunion.org.au

Scripture Union USA
PO Box 987, Valley Forge, PA 19482, USA
Website: www.scriptureunion.org

Scripture quotations are from the Contemporary English Version © American Bible Society 1991, 1992, 1995, Anglicisations © British and Foreign Bible Society 1997, or from the Good News Bible © American Bible Society 1992, both published in the UK by HarperCollins*Publishers*. Used by permission. Or New International Version © International Bible Society, Anglicisations © 2001, used by permission of Hodder and Stoughton Limited.

British Library Cataloguing-in-Publication Data.
A catalogue record of this book is available from the British Library.

Printed and bound in China by 1010 Printing International Ltd
All DVD introductions are taken from the original script for the video, *David the shepherd boy* by Mary Hawes
Cover illustration by Brent Clark
Internal illustrations by Brent Clark
Cover and internal template design by Kevin Wade of kwgraphicdesign.
Internal layout by Helen Jones

Scripture Union is an international Christian charity, working with churches in more than 130 countries, providing resources to bring the good news of Jesus Christ to children, young people and families and to encourage them to develop spiritually through the Bible and prayer.

As well as our network of volunteers, staff and associates who run holidays, church-based events and school Christian groups, we produce a wide range of publications and support those who use our resources through training programmes.

Target Challenge is an *eye level* club programme, part of *eye level*, Scripture Union's project to catch up with children and young people who have yet to catch sight of Jesus.

For details of other *eye level* club resources and additional *Target Challenge* material visit: www.scriptureunion.org.uk/eyelevel

Dedication and thanks

To the children who enrich my life daily – Millie and Hannah.
May you discover, like David, that the Lord is your Shepherd.

To Vickie Price and the team at Kings Road Church, Berkhamsted.
Thank you for your creative input, prayers and willingness to trial
Target Challenge. We had a great time!

Contents page

Starting out

Sessions

Starting out

How to use Target Challenge

David was the shepherd boy who became Israel's greatest king. He was a man of action and a brave warrior but also a poet and musician, who loved nothing better than to worship God. *Target Challenge* introduces children to David, the shepherd king, through action-packed adventure stories and multi-sensory activities, with plenty of space for quiet reflection. The final session makes the link to David's descendant, Jesus, the 'Good Shepherd' and King of kings.

The material is suitable for a midweek club, weekend event or school Christian group – we hope it will hit the mark for yours! On page 18 there are suggestions for how the material can be adapted for a 20 minute lunchtime club when time is short!
Target challenge has also been designed to follow on from *Champion's Challenge,* the holiday club programme that uses Luke's Gospel, and was created for those wanting a sporting theme, especially in the light of the Olympics. Accurately hitting a target is an element of several sports (as well as being a sport David 'played'), so *Target Challenge* provides an appropriate indoors environment with a sporting connection.

The aim of Target Challenge

Life in the 21st century is full of noise and activity. Our children have never known a world without mobile phones or computers. The aim of *Target Challenge* is to create a calm, quiet space where everyone can learn about prayer in an experiential way, meet with God, and respond by welcoming the King of kings. The activities make very few assumptions about children's previous knowledge of the Bible or experience of a Christian community.

At the heart of *Target Challenge* is the intention that children have fun as they build relationships with other children, with adult leaders and with God. In this context, leaders can naturally share Jesus and what he means to them, and the part that prayer and stillness play in their lives. Over the weeks trust will grow, as will the questions children ask and the answers they find. Our prayer is that the Holy Spirit will be at work in the life of each child who attends, whether this is the first time they have been part of anything Christian or they are already part of a church community.

How the programme works

This eight-week programme is designed to go with the *Target Challenge* DVD (six four- to seven-minute illustrated stories that focus on the early part of David's life). The material was originally produced by Scripture Union as the *David the Shepherd King* video which you may find available in your church video archives! If you do not want to use the DVD, it is possible to use this material but you will need to tell the story to complement the reading of the story in the Bible. Suggestions for this have been included in the first six sessions. The DVD has six episodes to go with the first six sessions. The final two sessions take a different approach to telling the story.

Each session is divided into three parts – 'Target practice' (preparation), 'Finding focus' (exploration), 'Hitting the spot' (application). Choose some or all of the activities on offer in each part. The times in brackets for each one indicate how long to allow, whether you're running a short half-hour session, or a longer one of an hour and a half or more. But do recognise that the unique nature of your group means these timings are not 100 per cent applicable.

What makes *Target Challenge* different from other programmes? Children's lives are so busy and distracted that the concept of rest and reflection can be quite alien to them. This programme is intended to give children a space on a regular basis where they can have time to be creative (without the necessary targets that accompany school creativity), time for personal reflection and time just to 'be'. The trial of the programme was welcomed by several parents who were concerned about the demands placed upon their children – these were largely parents who were not part of a local church. *Target Challenge* may therefore meet not only the needs of the children but also the desires of parents.

The prayer pod which has a peaceful, calm feel to it is available for the children to use at any point. For more details see page 10. Children learn in lots of different ways, so *Target Challenge* provides a range of multi-sensory activities which, overall, will connect with most children. These activities use all the children's senses at various stages in the programme. Leaders may not connect with all approaches, but do recognise that many of the children will have different learning styles from the adults present. Schools certainly encourage using different learning styles.

Target Challenge also aims to help every child make progress on their spiritual journey towards a living relationship with God, recognising that the starting point will be different for each. The take-home sheets evolved during the trial (see page 65). They were given to non-church children's parents so they would know what was being done in the club. They proved to be a very useful way of making first contact with parents and then maintaining that.

What's in the programme?

There are eight *Target Challenge* session outlines – the final session brings together the whole series (and could be used as the basis for an all-age multi-sensory service):

The shepherd boy: 1 Samuel 17:12–15; 16:19,21,23 (Introducing David)

The future king: 1 Samuel 16:1–13 (Samuel anoints David)

The giant: 1 Samuel 17:4–11,32–37,40–51 (David and Goliath)

The singer: 1 Samuel 18:6–16 (Saul's jealousy of David)

The friends: 1 Samuel 20:1–3,12,13,17–23,35–42 (Saul tries to kill David; David and Jonathan)

The outlaw: 1 Samuel 24:1–11,16–20 (David spares Saul's life)

King David: 2 Samuel 5:1–4,17–20; 6:1–5 (David becomes king over Israel; the Ark brought to Jerusalem)

David's King: Matthew 21:1–10 (The Triumphal Entry)

✸ Part 1: Target practice
(5–30 minutes)

'Target practice' is a selection of fun activities that introduce the session's theme. They involve movement, games, refreshments and action – a good way for everyone to get to know each other better and let off steam at the beginning of a session. Vary the time according to the mood of the children as they arrive, the type of venue you have, the number of helpers and the time available for your session.

If your group is meeting at lunchtime, you will need to be very clear as to what you can do since time is short. Children need a break in the middle of the day so a relaxed atmosphere and non-school type activities are called for. Suggestions for using the programme for just 20-minutes are on page 18.

If your group is meeting straight after school the children may need to run around and let off steam, or they may be tired out! They will certainly need some refreshments.

After their evening meal they will be more relaxed. On Saturday or Sunday the conditions will be different again, with more time available, other competing activities and maybe some children who are staying with the parent they don't live with during the week.

You will have to assess what best introduces them to the *Target Challenge* atmosphere. However, don't let this part of the programme go on too long. Allow enough time for 'Finding focus' and 'Hitting the spot'. Ideas for those first few minutes, or whenever you might have a bit of extra time, are on page 14. Whatever you do, make sure that the group feels properly welcomed and comfortable. 'Target practice' ends with a short relaxation/Bible meditation exercise, 'Being still'.

In each session there are ideas for preparing and eating food together. This is a great way to build relationships and have fun. Obviously you need to decide what to do, after consultation with parents. You do not want to spoil the appetite of children before a meal and they won't be hungry after a meal. Also find out about food allergies and make sure the children have washed their hands before eating or preparing food!

Dart ball and skittles
See Session 1 on how to set this up. Take time to set it up properly if you are going to do this every week. It will help create continuity as well as keeping the link with the sports/*Champion's Challenge* theme.

Part 2: Finding focus
(10–15 minutes)
'Finding focus' is the place to find the detail of each session's theme. Use the script and suggested props to introduce the DVD clip and then read the Bible verses with the children. You can choose from a range of activities in 'Hitting the spot' to develop the theme.

Children do watch a lot of television and DVDs but they may not often watch and share a programme with others, including interested adults. Even at school there will be a definite education focus to any television viewing. So this could be quite a unique experience for them.

Remember that some children find reading hard or just don't like it. Reading the Bible may appear hard work or boring, but it doesn't have to be. After all, this is God's unique Word to us. Be imaginative in how you use it. Children can listen to it being read, they can act it out, draw it, memorise it, set it to music, pick out key words and so on. But some will want to read it. Bible reading is deliberately central to this programme. That is why the Bible passages are included in each session with significant highlighted words or phrases, a quiz suggestion or ideas for bringing the Bible alive. You may want to photocopy some of the passages or produce them on an acetate or PowerPoint slide. The Bible verses have been reproduced from the Contemporary English Version and used with permission. This version is especially good for reading out loud. Whatever version of the Bible you use, make sure it is child-friendly and doesn't look old or out of date!

The Bible could be part of a child's life-long after you have left them! Your enthusiasm for God's Word will be infectious. Make sure that your own Bible is in evidence and that you make it clear that the stories you are exploring come from the Bible.

Part 3: Hitting the spot
(15–45 minutes)
'Hitting the spot' suggests activities to consolidate the learning, leaning towards reflective, multi-sensory exercises and creative prayer. Select activities according to the size of the group, the ages of the children and the help you have available.

Each week's art and craft creations will help stimulate prayer and discussion the following week, if either left *in situ* or reinstalled by leaders and children during 'Target practice'. At the very least you will want to create a display on a noticeboard in the room or hall where you meet, including any artwork done by the children, and perhaps some key words from each week.

Ending

Make sure that you end properly and as calmly as possible. Try to say goodbye to each child personally. The children will be more likely then to remember what they have learnt and be aware of the positive relationships there have been in *Target Challenge*. Friendships made with other children and leaders may be the most important part of *Target Challenge*.

Reminders

Target Challenge sessions work as single sessions but are designed to be part of a programme. To help the children be aware of this and make connections from one week to the next, updating the noticeboard or display of children's work each week is vital. Praying the STOP prayers together each week will also bring elements of continuity.

Other regular features

The prayer pod
The prayer pod should be prepared every week with a peaceful, calm feel to it, in an accessible, public place, preferably in a corner or alcove. If possible it needs to be large enough to accommodate all the group towards the end of

each session. It is not just for specific prayer but a place for quiet if a child wants some space, feels overwhelmed or wants to sleep! You could include cushions, beanbags, comfy chairs, drapes, fairy lights (placed out of children's reach), books with stories about Jesus, inspiring pictures and Bible verses in your prayer pod. Each session will provide more of the children's own work to display here so this area will grow as the eight weeks progress. One adult leader will need to keep an eye on any child/children who come to use the corner. They may want to chat, or even pray with someone else.

An art and craft area

A regular art and craft area/table would be helpful. A washing line and pegs are useful for displaying pictures and drying paintings quickly and easily.

Take-home sheets

If you're giving children a 'take-home sheet' for parents and carers to read, remember to have a pile ready by the door, along with the Learn and remember verse cards. A template for this is on page 65. It does not have to be sophisticated in its layout, but clear! Keep the number of words down to a minimum!

The purpose of such a sheet is to keep parents informed of what is going on in the club and what else is happening within the church community. You might want to include a brief summary of the session's story, the Learn and remember verse, the theme of the session written in language that a non-church person can understand, requests for help or equipment, and an indication of what will be looked at next session. You might also want to include a puzzle for the children, which may mean they are more likely to deliver it home!

Getting to know you

✳ Building relationships

The children you'll meet at *Target Challenge* live in a fast-moving, sophisticated, technology-orientated world, dominated by screens. There is so much 'stuff' demanding their attention. Rather than trying to compete with that sort of environment, offer them what they are often missing elsewhere – real communication. Concentrate on the unique opportunity you

have to build relationships; listen to them, talk with them, and give them time as you show them God's love in action. That way they will get to know you, each other and Jesus on their *Target Challenge* adventure, and have a great time too!

✳ Top tips for sharing Jesus with children

• **Build strong friendships.** Be genuinely interested in their lives, homes, hobbies, what happens at school. These friendships will be bridges across which Jesus can walk! Ensure that these children know that you appreciate and respect them.

• **Be informed** about what is happening at school and home – it's useful to be in the know about sports days, class excursions or family events, and these may explain why the children are excited or tired, or both!

• **Get to know the children's families.** Understand their home lives, and help their parents (or whoever is responsible for their care) know what they are learning. Children can never be divorced from their home backgrounds. Avoid talking about Mum and Dad. It's best to refer to Mum *or* Dad or even, 'whoever looks after you at home'.

• **Remember birthdays**, or ask someone else to take on the responsibility of noting dates and preparing cards, perhaps for the other children to sign.

• **Do as you say!** The children need to see you model what you teach them. Your friendship with Jesus matters. How else will the children see what it means in practice to be in a relationship with him?

• **Encourage everyone to join in,** adults and children alike. Create a 'we're in this together' feel to the sessions, rather than 'them and us'. Avoid organising activities that adults stand and watch. Relax, have fun and learn with the children – *'Aim to give children the best hour of their week!'* Dave Connelly, Frontline Church.

• **Mind your language!** Avoid jargon words (eg sin, grace or churchy words) and explain what you mean by things like prayer.

• **Use illustrations from everyday life** to explain concepts. Jesus taught complex truths in simple ways, eg 'You can't see wind, but you can see the effects that it has; it's the same with the Holy Spirit'. You will need to think about this before the club begins.

• **Grow the children's confidence with the Bible** and explain how to read it. Why don't we often start at page 1? How do we use the Contents page? (Younger children find this very hard.) What are the differences between chapters and verses, or the Old and New Testaments? How do you explain that the Bible is one big story – God's story – in different bits? Find out more about the Bible in *The Story of the Book* (see page 79).

• **Talk about Jesus,** rather than God, where possible. The Gospels give us clear pictures of what he is like and these are far easier to grasp than the idea of God being 'up there' but invisible. Children have some very woolly ideas about God, but there is less room for manoeuvre when it comes to Jesus! *Target Challenge* is based on the Old Testament but Jesus is naturally introduced as you share your faith.

• **Apply the Bible teaching appropriately:** When thinking about how God protected David, ask about times when children need God's help and protection, for instance when someone is being unkind to them.

• **Allow children to make responses** that are appropriate for them, their understanding and their backgrounds. Don't rush straight in with, 'Do you want to follow Jesus?' That should be a decision that lasts for life, and they need to recognise what it entails. For many children, there are a number of commitments as their understanding grows.

• **Have fun together!** The children need to catch something of the 'life in all its fullness' that Jesus spoke about.

Child protection

Why do you need a child protection policy? The policy is there to guide you. It helps protect children that come to your sessions from harm, and it will protect you.

Most churches have a child protection policy so make sure you are familiar with it. Hopefully there is a child protection representative who will guide you if you have any questions. It is the church's responsibility to keep up to date with changes in best practice.

If your church doesn't have a policy, contact CCPAS for advice on how to set one up at www.ccpas.co.uk

⊛ **Key things to remember:**

• All volunteers need to be appointed in an appropriate manner, including CRB checks.

Plan ahead because these take time to come through but are vital.
• Brief all volunteers with regards to what they must do if a child discloses abuse.
• Have a registration form for each child, including medical details and consent in case a parent cannot be contacted in an emergency.
• Have enough leaders to children. The recommended ratio for a group is:

0 to 2 years – 1 adult for 3 children
2 to 3 years – 1 adult for 4 children
3 to 8 years – 1 adult for 8 children
8 years and over – 2 adults for every 20 children/young people (1 male, 1 female, plus 1 additional adult for every extra 10).

• Make sure there has been a risk assessment made for activities.
• Ask to see your church's Health and Safety Policy, especially if you are using a kitchen.
• If you are preparing food, make sure you are aware of any children with food allergies.
• Ensure all your volunteers know what standard of behaviour is expected of them.
• Make sure you know what your church's special needs policy is.

Helping children build a relationship with God

Target Challenge focuses on the importance of communicating with God in a variety of ways: hearing from him, speaking to him, meditating on him through the Bible. Seeds are being sown about communicating with God. Since the programme is based on the Old Testament there is not such an emphasis upon a relationship with Jesus, apart from the final session which connects David with Jesus, a greater king. But inevitably, there will be opportunities for leaders to share what knowing God and Jesus means in reality. As children participate in the reflective and prayer activities, they may ask to find out more about entering into a relationship with God, the good shepherd. Be ready to help them.
• They rarely need long explanations, just simple answers to questions.

- Talk to them in a place where you can be seen by others in line with your child protection policy.
- Never put pressure on children to respond in a particular way, just help them take one step closer to Jesus when they are ready. We don't want them to respond just to please us!
- Remember, many children make a commitment to Jesus, followed by further commitments as they mature and their understanding grows.
- Many children just need a bit of help to say what they want to say to God. Here is a suggested prayer they could use to make a commitment to Jesus:

> **Dear God,**
> **Thank you that you love me.**
> **I'm sorry for all the things I've done wrong, which you did not want me to do.**
> **Thank you that Jesus your Son came to live on earth and understands what it's like to be a child.**
> **Thank you that he died on the cross for me and that means I can be forgiven.**
> **Please forgive me.**
> **Please be my friend and help me each day to please you.**
> **Amen.**

For more details on nurturing faith read *Top Tips on Encouraging faith to grow* (SU) 2008. Available from SU Mail Order Tel: 0845 0706 006

What to do after Target Challenge

✸ Step one – time to think

Hopefully, *Target Challenge* has made you think about how you run activities and reach out to children in your community. Before the end of the *Target Challenge* series, plan a review with anyone who helped. Be as honest as you can and dream dreams!
- What did the children enjoy about *Target Challenge*?
- What was different compared with your previous activities for children?

- Were there more small-group activities? How did they work?
- Was there more Bible input than before?
- What worked really well or didn't work?
- What did the leaders enjoy?
- What did you discover about each other's gifts for working with children? Was there an unknown storyteller or someone especially good at welcoming children?

Write down the most important answers. Talk about what you should do next.

✸ Step two – moving on

Don't be afraid to develop what you provide for children. If *Target Challenge* encouraged you to run a midweek or Saturday club for the first time and it worked, plan to carry on. You may need extra help, especially if some people can't commit themselves weekly. Perhaps you could continue your club next term or maybe a monthly Saturday/Sunday special, using another Scripture Union programme.

Discuss how you might contact new children. What are your links with the local school(s) or neighbourhood groups? Could you publicise your group through the local paper or library? How could the children who already come be encouraged to bring their friends? Just how many more children can you cope with?

✸ Step three – building on *Target Challenge*

One of the aims of *Target Challenge* is to bring children who don't usually have much contact with a Christian community into a Christian activity. If this worked for you, build on the final *Target Challenge* session and get to know the children's families by running a parents' special event. Family games work well, either games to play within families, or families competing against one another. Any family activity that offers food will be popular! Alternatively, some churches have explored parenting groups. In one place a church football team has developed from fathers of children who started coming to a church children's club. Be imaginative and find out what other churches in your area have done. Maybe you could do something together.

Whatever you do, try to maintain contact with children, to sustain and grow your relationships. You may wish to visit them at home, to deliver a birthday card or to let parents know the starting date for next term, or to invite families to a family event or special service such as a carol service. If you do home visits make sure parents are happy for you to come and contact them to arrange a time for your visit.

Other programmes
Streetwise, Awesome!, Clues2Use, Rocky Road and *High Five,* eight-session eyelevel programmes similar in aim and design to *Target Challenge,* are also available from good local Christian bookshops or from SU Mail Order: Scripture Union Mail Order, PO Box 5148, Milton Keynes MLO, MK2 2YX
Tel: 0845 07 06 006 Fax: 01908 856020
Web: www.scriptureunion.org.uk

Extra activities

 **Guess who?**
(5–10 minutes)

What you need
• The interviews the children and adults recorded in week 1

What you do
Pick a couple of interviews (in the first couple of weeks it might be best to choose from the leaders' ones). Tell the children they need to guess who gave these answers. Read out hobbies, favourite sandwich filling and 'job' from the 'interview' so everyone can guess who it is.

 Song
(5–10 minutes)

What you need
• A CD, tape or DVD with children's songs on
• A CD, tape or DVD player

What you do
With a few spare minutes, you could teach the children a simple song that's based on a Psalm. Make sure that you are not putting words into the mouths of children that they do not understand or mean. This is especially important when working with unchurched children. Using a DVD can be good because it provides them with something visual.

 **Prayer shields**

(5–10 minutes)
from Session 4 onwards
Do this activity in the prayer pod.

What you need
• Shields cut out of paper (left over from Session 3) stacked in the prayer corner, easily accessible
• Pencils/pens

What you do
Remind the children about the prayer shields they made in Session 3 and explain that they can always write another prayer shield if there's something that seems like a big problem or a difficult situation that they or someone they know is facing. Assure them that the leaders will keep praying about these things (so long as that is true!). If the child allows, use any new written prayers during STOP, so that everyone can pray together. Review how God may have answered *shield prayers* from previous weeks, during any spare time in a session.

4 Psalm 24:1 Nature Table
(5–10 minutes)

If planning to do this, ask children to bring something from the natural world with them. Make sure leaders bring lots of examples too, just in case…!

What you need
• A low table or box (in the prayer pod)
• A cloth to drape over the box
• Children's examples of 'nature' supplemented by what leaders have brought (eg stones, seashells, leaves, feathers, flowers, driftwood, bark, acorns)
• Digital camera (optional)
• Paper and painting/drawing resources

What you do
Help the children to find a creative way to display their things from nature in the prayer pod. Could you incorporate Psalm 24:1, 'The earth is the Lᴏʀᴅ's and everything in it' (NIV) written out in a decorative way? While working on the display, talk with the children about why they chose the particular things they brought in, or which items they like best. What do they like about these things? What do the different objects remind them of? Some children might want to do a drawing or paint a picture inspired by nature to add to the display.
    An alternative to making a conventional 'nature table' would be to make some 'natural

art', using the objects to create interesting shapes and patterns and then take digital photos, either to print and display next session or to use in a slide show. This would work particularly well in summer, as you could make your natural art in the open air (as long as you have a safe outdoor space to use).

✸5 Bible Storyboard
(10–20 minutes)
This activity is more suited to a smaller group including some older children. It works best visually with bold drawings using chunky pens on a long roll of paper. Draw equal sized boxes along the paper, one for each scene.

What you need
- Flip chart or roll of white paper (even the back of an unwanted roll of wallpaper)
- Marker pens
- Photocopied Bible passage for that particular session, marked up into shorter passages, each containing one part of the action

What you do
Introduce the way comics tell a story using pictures and just a few words, then tell the children you're going to retell today's story about David in the same way. You will need volunteers to do the drawing. Ask one (or a couple taking it in turns) of the older children to read out the Bible story scene by scene, with a pause between each scene. While the whole Bible Storyboard group listen, the volunteer 'cartoonists' do quick sketches to represent each part of the story. The children should take it in turns to draw a scene until you've got a cartoon version of the whole thing. Afterwards, you may want to show this to the rest of the group and talk about what you've learned.

✸6 Someone special
(5–10 minutes)
Younger children will need help with the writing. The framed style of mirror, with some added adhesive decorations, would be more fun for this age group.

What you need
- Small unframed mirrors – cardboard backed, **not** made of glass (bulk buy available from art and craft shops)
- EITHER – a collection of cardboard frames to use with the mirrors; paint and marker pens
- OR – special 'glass paint' pens
- Sticky tape

- Silver string and scissors
- A finished example for the children to see, with the words written very clearly for young children to copy. The words could be a short Bible verse or the phrase '_____is special to God'.

What you do
If the children are going to use frames, start by painting them. You will need to let the frames dry before the children can write on them and finally slip the mirror inside.

If the children are not going to frame the mirrors, they can use the special 'glass paint' pens to write the words directly onto the mirrors, and maybe add decoration. They should do all their writing and decoration round the edges, though, if they want to be able to see themselves in it!

Finally, attach lengths of string to the back of the frame or mirror with sticky tape so it can be hung.

✸7 Play dough or tin foil modelling
(5–10 minutes)

What you need
- EITHER - a large batch of home-made play dough (much cheaper than the bought stuff) For recipe instructions go to www.topmarks.co.uk/Parents/Recipe.aspx
- OR - a roll of tin foil

What you do
Ask the children to use the play dough or tin foil to model something that represents either their favourite character or their 'best bit' of the story so far. This is a good way to recap on what you've been learning and to find out what's made the biggest impression!

Alternatively the children could use the play dough/tin foil for self-expression. As they work, they may want to talk about what they've been thinking about.

✸8 Margarine tub drums and shakers
(5–10 minutes)
These would complement the elastic band harps of Session 4

What you need
- A collection of margarine tubs with their lids
- Pencils to use as drumsticks
- Pasta to put in shakers

- Sticky tape to attach the lids permanently
- Stickers/glue/things for decorating the drums and shakers

What you do
Each child decorates a margarine tub and either puts some pasta inside for a shaker, or leaves it empty for a drum. Attach the lids using sticky tape. The children either play their drum using pencil drumsticks, or shake their shaker. Can they listen to each other's instruments and rhythms to make some music together? Can they beat out someone's name for everyone to guess? What sort of sounds do their different instruments make? What sort of mood do they think they could create with these instruments/this music?

Games

Target Challenge has been written to help children's leaders explore a more reflective style of running a children's club. However, you may have children in your club who really need to let off steam and enjoy energetic activities. You may also be running *Target Challenge* as a follow-up to the holiday club programme *Champion's Challenge*, which had a sporty theme. You may want to include a significant games element to your programme, more than just the dart ball and skittles suggested in the session. That is why the games below have been included. They have been adapted from those suggested in *Champion's Challenge*. Do use them as appropriate.

As with dart ball, the children are not working to beat anyone else's score, just their own. These activities need a leader per challenge to count/score. If possible, create and give out certificates for each child, naming the sports at which they have improved their personal best.

Choose any of the following. Include at least one marked * as these are the 'special sports' for children with special needs.

⊛1 Tin can alley *

What you need
- Soft small ball (tennis ball size)
- 10 empty soft drinks cans in a pyramid
- A chair

What you do
Sit on a chair to throw. Knock down as many cans as possible with the ball. Score by counting the number of cans in three throws, or the number of throws needed to demolish the stack.

⊛2 Standing jump

What you need
- Tape measure (metric)
- Mark on floor for start point

What you do
Measure the distance jumped, feet together, from a standing position – no run up!

⊛3 Skipping

What you need
- Skipping rope
- A watch with a second hand

What you do
Count the consecutive skips in 30 seconds.

⊛4 Walk in the dark *

What you need
- Chairs
- Blindfold

What you do
Walk through a course of chairs, whilst blindfolded. Have a leader to guide the children and take great care!

⊛5 Bounce! *

What you need
- Tennis racket and ball
- A watch with a second hand

What you do
Count the number of consecutive bounces of a ball on a tennis racket in 30 seconds. Can be done sitting down in order to make it a *challenge.

⊛6 Buzz off! *

What you need

- A metal frame connected to a battery, with hand-held hoop to be passed over it. You may know someone who has one of these or a small one can be bought quite cheaply.

What you do

Score either on maximum distance achieved or time taken to complete it without buzzing.

⊛7 Hop on!

What you need

- A watch with a second hand

What you do

Count consecutive hops on either leg. Allow 30 seconds per person.

⊛8 Squat thrusts

What you need

- A watch with a second hand

What you do

Count the number of squat thrusts (hands on floor, legs straight out, then feet jumped up towards hands) in 30 seconds.

Other games

(to be played in a large space with the whole group, well supervised)

⊛1 Under the posts

Ask the children to spread out around the room. Choose one child to chase the other children (two children if you have large numbers). When a child is 'tagged' they must stand with their arms out at shoulder level. They are 'freed' by another child running round them, under their outstretched arms. At regular intervals, pick another child to be 'it'.

⊛2 Coach is coming

Ask the children to spread out around the room. Explain that when you call out certain names they have to respond with an action as quickly as possible. If they are the last to do it, they are out. Name the ends of the room as 'home' and 'away' and the sides as 'tee' and 'hole' –when

you call these names the children must run to that part of the room. If you call out 'sprint', they must run on the spot; 'hole in one', they sit on the floor; 'ace', they run round in a circle on the spot, with their arms in the air and 'coach is coming', they stand still.

Where possible avoid elimination down to the last person as children who are out become quickly bored.

⊛3 Sporting corners

In each corner put a large sign with a picture or name of a different sport. Make four small cards of the same sports and fold them in half. Play music and get the children to dance or jog around. When the music stops they must jog to a corner and stay in it. Read out the name of a sport from one of the small cards and whoever is in that corner is 'out' for one go.

⊛4 Parachute games

There are many games that can be played inside and outside with a parachute. For some brilliant ideas visit www.funandgames.org/games.html

Families' ministry

Of course, children belong to their wider family and in running *Target Challenge* you will meet different family members and may hear lots about them too! It is important to keep parents and carers informed about what is going on in the club, which is one of the reasons for having the take-home sheets. Welcoming and saying goodbye properly will help you to keep in contact with families. Invite parents to come to the final session and ensure they know what is planned after the programme is completed.

You may want to explore follow-up events for the whole family. Parenting courses are frequently a valuable activity to offer. The sporting theme lends itself to an all-age event, such as a mini-Olympics or a tenpin bowling outing for all the family. *Champion's Challenge* includes ideas for building relationships with the whole family. For more ideas on family ministry read *Top Tips on Growing faith with families* (SU) 2007. Available from SU Mail Order Tel: 0845 0706 006

Suggestions for a short lunchtime session

You will need to be selective because there won't be time to do all the options in each session. You may choose to take two weeks for each session, spread over two terms with a review at the start of the second term. Do use the DVD if at all possible but there are story-telling or Bible interaction suggestions. The food and family members' suggestions will probably not apply to your situation. Aim to have some routine for each session such as dartball. If you begin with this, it doesn't matter if there are 2 or 22 children there at the start. Remember, children need to unwind after morning school with something a bit different from what they have been doing all morning.

Session 1 The shepherd boy

Badges
Dart ball or similar game to improve skills over the next weeks
Being still
Introduce David
Short story of David playing the harp for the king
Bible passage with 'Who am I?' chart
Learn and remember verse

Session 2 The future king

Dart ball or Signatures game
Being still
Introduce David
Tell the story of David being chosen
Bible passage and quiz
Learn and remember verse

Session 3 The giant

Dart ball or catapults
Being still
Introduce David
Read/tell story of David and Goliath
Bible passage with game (if room)
Prayer shields
Learn and remember verse

Session 4 The singer

Elastic band harps
Being still
Introduce David
Read Bible passage with interaction
Create psalm picture
Song of praise as a prayer
Learn and remember verse

Session 5 The friends

Cotton bud javelins
Being still
Introduce David
Tell story or read Bible passage
Learn and remember verse
Prayer web

Session 6 The outlaw

Dart ball or pin the tail on the sheep
Being still
Introduce David
Bible passage and quiz
Learn and remember verse

Session 7 King David

Dart ball or hopscotch
Being still
Bible passage and drama
Praise workshop
Learn and remember verse

Session 8 David's king

(Aim to review the whole series)
Dart ball or penalty shoot-out
Being still
Bible passage and drama
Who is in your family?/Gathering up the sheep (pre-prepared)
Learn and remember verse

For more information on running a club in a primary school at lunchtime or straight after school, visit the Supa Clubs website: www.scriptureunion.org.uk/2908.id

Session 1
The shepherd boy

Target practice

Welcome the children to *Target Challenge*. Introduce yourself and any other adult helpers. Be very organised at the beginning to ensure everyone gets a badge made. Don't delay on beginning craft activities. As the children finish their badges, they can drift to the things that are set up all the time – dart ball and skittles (see page 20).

If you are not going to make badges with the children, ensure that each child wears a sticker so that you can remember names and create a sense of belonging. This is especially important if it is the first time you have run a club like this.

 Snack – shepherd's picnic
(5–20 minutes)

What you need
- Picnic rugs or blankets – be careful of slippery floors
- Cuddly toy lambs (optional)!
- Paper plates or kitchen towel squares and plastic knives
- Picnic ingredients: sliced bread, spread, grated cheese, jam, or, if it's after a meal, a smaller snack, eg crackers and soft cheese.
- Drinks

What you do
Set the scene to create a picnic 'mood' in the place where you meet. Ask children to spread picnic rugs on the floor. Put the food, plates and plastic knives in the middle of the 'table' so that children can take it in turns to assemble their own sandwiches, a few at a time. Encourage adult helpers to chat with the children while you sit on the blankets to eat your refreshments. In preparation for the sheep topic, you could ask whether anyone has ever been to a farm/seen a lamb/watched a shepherd rounding up the sheep.

2 Target Challenge badges
(10–20 minutes)

What you need
- A demonstration model!
- Card cut into circles of approx 5 cm diameter (draw round a glass for the template)
- Safety pins
- Strong tape, such as masking tape, to attach the pins to the card
- Target template on page 76 the same size as the card circles (photocopied for each child onto coloured paper but on a pale setting, so it's just a background)
- Selection of art materials, eg glitter, shiny paper, stickers, coloured pens, gel pens
- Glue sticks
- Scissors
- Aprons to cover school uniform if doing messy crafts

If you have a badge machine, use it with the badge cut-outs supplied by the manufacturer (they will need to be a specific size) to make your badges look smart and last longer. In this case the photocopied target templates will need to be a few millimetres larger than the card circles they're being stuck to as the machine tucks the edges over to attach the two. Please follow the manufacturer's instructions!

What you do
Give each child a cardboard circle, a safety pin, a small piece of masking tape and a target template. Place the right side of the safety pin in the middle of the cardboard circle and stick it down with tape. Each child writes their name on a target template, adding decoration (but keeping it within the circle). Cut the target to size and stick it to the front of the badge (the youngest children may need help with this). They can wear their badges every week, if you collect them in at the end of each session.

Bible
1 Samuel 17:12–15; 16:19,21,23

Aim
To introduce children to David as a boy, who was brave when faced with danger and trusted God when he was afraid.

God listens to us when we pray, which means that when we're frightened or worried, we can tell God about it and ask for his help.

Checklist
- A prayer pod
- An art and craft area/table
- Take-home sheets
- Material for your chosen activities
- Make a note of any food allergies when signing children in!

1

World of a child

Children from a non-church background will probably not know much about David or what life was like 3,000 years ago in Israel. Make sure that you do not assume that they are familiar with David and his background.

This is an important session for setting the scene and the atmosphere for the following sessions, as well as laying down ground rules.

⊕3 Dart ball
(up to 25 minutes)

What you need
- Dart ball
- Personal 'target practice' scoresheets for each child (see page 76 for the template)
- Dart ball is a safe dartboard game which uses Velcro with fluffy balls and an inflatable target. If you can't find/don't have Dart ball you could cut some holes out of a piece of firm cardboard and write different scores over each hole to set this up like a fairground stall with 3 bean bags or soft balls for children to throw through.

What you do
Set this up against a wall every week, encouraging children to have a few practice shots and then each child has one 'proper' go, recording this score on their personal 'target practice' scoresheet, template on page 76. They can see if, with practise, they improve their aim over the eight weeks of *Target Challenge*. Children should hand in their scoresheets so you can sort them into alphabetical order ready to hand out again next week.

Note: additional games ideas can be found on pages 16 and 17.

⊕4 Skittles
(up to 25 minutes)

What you need
- A set of skittles and at least two balls (several sets if you're expecting lots of children)

What you do
See how many skittles each child can knock over with their two balls. Alternatively bring lots of balls and let them keep trying until all the skittles are knocked over. How many tries does it take?

⊕5 Being still exercise
(2–5 minutes)

What you need
- CD of instrumental music to play in background; CD player
- Rugs/mats

What you do
To draw the children together and calm them down at the end of 'Target practice', ask them to find a space on a rug on the floor. Now would be a good time to talk about the prayer pod and how they might use it. Explain about 'Being still' and how each week they're going to spend some time relaxing and being quiet and maybe hearing some words from the Bible to think about. Ask everyone to lie down on their backs and close their eyes for a relaxation exercise. This will involve consciously tensing and relaxing neck, shoulders, arms, hands, fingers, legs, feet, toes and then imagining all their limbs are very heavy, but resting on a soft, fluffy cloud or flying/floating to somewhere very nice. What can the children see/hear/touch/taste/smell? If possible, play them some harp music to show how soothing it is. When they've taken it all in, they can open their eyes and sit up gradually, staying where they can see the TV/projector screen for 'Finding focus'.

> ❻ *'Being still' was great, particularly with leaders happy to join in. There were a few giggles but everyone felt comfortable and enjoyed it – it set the mood really well for what was to follow.* ❾
> *Vickie*

Alternatively, you could play 'Sleeping lions'. Ask the children to lie on the floor as still as they possibly can for a game of 'Sleeping lions', a traditional children's party game. One of the leaders will be watching for movement – anyone who moves will be asked to join the 'watcher/s'. If the children are too good at this, telling jokes may make them start giggling and wriggling which hastens along the game! No need to wait until everyone's eliminated. Just congratulate the most convincing 'sleeping lions' when it's time to stop.

Finding focus

◖❶ Introduce David
(10–15 minutes)

What you need
- Dressing up clothes
- Who am I? chart; pens
- DVD and player (if using)

Explain that at each *Target Challenge* session, everyone will hear true stories about someone called David who started off as a shepherd boy, looking after sheep, and ended up as a king ruling all the people in two countries called Israel and Judah. We will also find out about David's God and how talking to him and singing praises to him was an important part of David's life, just as it can be for us.

Use a nativity costume or sheet and stripy tea towel to dress up one of the older children as David the shepherd boy. If possible, provide them with a shepherd's crook/staff, cuddly lamb, home-made 'box harp' (see page 75), and a catapult (or home-made sling – a hammock-shaped pouch of thick fabric with either end plaited). Tell the children that later on you will be interviewing 'David' and give the children a list of questions to complete, so that they can listen out for the answers in the introduction, DVD and Bible reading.

Read the following introduction as animatedly as you can, demonstrating the harp and sling in some way:

'From an early age, David worked for King Saul as 'armour bearer'. He helped him get dressed for battle, but also played the harp when Saul was feeling troubled.

David was also a shepherd boy. When he wasn't with King Saul, he looked after his father's sheep. Sheep are difficult to look after. They wander off and get into all sorts of scrapes. When they get lost the shepherd has to go after them and find them. He also has to protect them from wild animals. It could be a lonely and dangerous job, but David wasn't frightened because he trusted God to protect him. His big brothers didn't think much of David. They were too busy fighting the Philistine army to worry about little lambs. (The Philistines were enemies of God's people, the Israelites.)

David was a *good* shepherd and did his job well. When things were quiet he liked to practise two things: using his sling and playing his harp. His sling was like a catapult but without elastic because elastic hadn't been invented then. It was made of plaited wool and he would put a pebble in the middle, swing it round his head, let one side go and off would shoot the pebble to hit the target! It took a lot of skill; so did playing the harp. David's harp wasn't a big one like you might see in an orchestra today: it was small, like a little box with strings stretched across it. David used to strum his harp, making up songs, mainly in praise of God. But looking after a field full of sheep, David always had to be on his guard…'

Show the DVD
(If you are not using the DVD, tell the story of David being summoned to the king to play his harp. Discuss with the children what they would feel like being given such an important job for the king: Afraid? Proud? Fearful that the king would get fed up with them? Lonely? God was preparing David for what he was going to do in the future.)

Read the Bible passage
Photocopy as required the Bible passage on page 70 and the Who am I? chart on page 22. Read the passage together pausing to fill in David's Who am I? chart in pairs or small groups when a phrase comes up.

Finish filling in David's answers to the interview together (name, address, boy/girl, brothers/sisters, hobbies, job etc). With older children you could look up the references. Some of the answers listed below are speculative and will have to be filled in by the leader, with some explanation (eg age, birthday, favourite sandwich filling).

Name: David, son of Jesse (17:12)
Dad's or mum's name: Jesse – dad
Address: Bethlehem in Judah (17:12)
Age: I think I'm about 15? Everyone tells me I'm 'only a boy' (17:33,42)
Birthday: Not sure
Boy/girl: Boy (17:33)
Brothers/sisters: Seven brothers (17:12)
Hobbies (what you do for fun): Play the harp, write songs and practise with my sling and stones (16:18; 17:40)
Favourite sandwich filling: Cheese, like the soldiers. (David takes bread and cheese to the soldiers in Saul's army, 17:17,18)
Job (is there a job you'd like to do?): I'm a shepherd and an 'armour bearer' (I help the king get dressed for battle), but I'd like to be a great musician, a soldier or maybe even king! (16:21,23; 17:15)

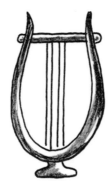

1

Who am I?

Name:

Dad's or mum's name:

Address:

Age:

Birthday:

Boy/girl:

Brothers/sisters:

Hobbies (what you do for fun):

Favourite sandwich filling:

Job (is there a job you'd like to do?):

Hitting the spot

You may want to split into smaller groups for these activities.

⊙1 Interview
(10–20 minutes)

Split into pairs and interview each other, writing down the answers if possible as a Who am I? chart from page 22. Adults should join in, pairing up with the youngest children to help them write – and answering the questions themselves. We particularly want an answer for everyone's hobbies, job and favourite sandwich filling. A spin-off game which can be used as a time-filler throughout the eight weeks would be reading out someone's hobbies, favourite sandwich and job from their list so everyone can guess who it is. Adults should do this at the beginning to show how it is done and to give children the chance to get to know the leaders.

⊙2 Things we fear
(10–20 minutes)

Start this activity in the art and craft corner, then move to the prayer pod.

What you need
- Art and craft materials
- Binoculars

What you do
Introduce this activity with a couple of questions and some discussion. What do you think might frighten you? Share with the children something that frightens you and how God has helped you to be brave in it – root it in real life. Ask the children what makes *them* afraid: thunderstorms, bullies, dogs, getting lost, something else? Encourage the children either to draw the thing that makes them frightened, or to write about it. Then move to the prayer pod.

Look at the pictures they've drawn through binoculars – their fears look HUGE. Now talk about how they think God will help them not to be afraid. What ideas do they have? Encourage them to bring their fears to God in prayer. 'Lord God, you know .... makes me frightened. Please help me to trust you. Amen.'

Finally, look through the binoculars the other way and see how tiny and unthreatening the fears now appear.

⊙3 Learn and remember verse
(5–15 minutes)

What you need
- A large STOP sign
- Shawls, soft scarves or wraps
- Poster/OHP of Psalm 17:8 – 'Hide me in the shadow of your wings.'
- Small copies of the Learn and remember verse on page 66 for the children to take home

What you do
Gather all the children in the prayer pod, explaining that when they see the STOP sign it means it's time to sit down there together. Explain that every week there'll be a short Bible verse to learn by heart for the next week.

Encourage the children to think about what this verse means and, possibly, to spend time praying. Now would be the best time to explain what prayer is, helping the children understand that we can talk to God about anything and that he always listens.

Read Psalm 17:8 out loud, with the OHP or poster visible. Talk about God's protection being like a shawl: he wraps his love around us. Let them try wrapping soft scarves or wraps around themselves, thinking about how God protects and surrounds us with his love. He's like a mother hen wrapping her wings round her little chicks to protect them from harm and keep them warm.

Repeat the Learn and remember verse several times, reading it all together. Don't forget to include the reference with it each time.

You'll need to gauge your group as to whether you can introduce prayer in the first session. But if you do want to, explain how STOP can help us know what to pray, because it stands for:

      Sorry
      Thank you
      Others
      Please

If you want to pray now, you can incorporate this week's themes:

Sorry (for things we've done that hurt or upset other people)
Thank you (for the good things God has given us, like new friends at *Target Challenge*)
Others (do we know people who are poorly or afraid and need help and protection from God?)
Please (hide me in the shadow of your wings and keep me safe)
Amen! (Everyone can join in with a loud Amen)

Make sure that you say goodbye to each child individually and, if possible, talk with the person who has come to collect each child.

1

'Hide me in the shadow of your wings.'

Psalm 17:8

Session 2
The future king

Target practice

Welcome the children to *Target Challenge* and give them their badges or name stickers to wear. Introduce yourself and any other adult helpers to any newcomers, and help them to make a badge. It's an opportunity to get to know or reassure them, to make them feel special. See Session 1 for the list of instructions for 'what you need' and 'what you do'.

Give out any notices and mention any children who have had birthdays since you last met. If some children arrive early they could start laying the banqueting table, or decorating frames – the sooner the better as they may take a while to dry.

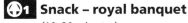 **Snack – royal banquet**
(10–20 minutes)

What you need
- A long table with chairs around it
- A long, dark red or purple tablecloth or a roll of white paper to use as table covering
- Decorations: candlesticks (with unlit candles), flowers/greenery, a large bunch of grapes in a 'silver' (kitchen foil covered) fruit bowl
- Paper plates
- Party finger food: crisps, cocktail sausages, chocolate biscuits, bite-sized cakes etc – if it's after dinner, scale it down, perhaps to just a cake or biscuit for each child
- Drinks (blackcurrant squash in plastic wine glasses or paper cups)

What you do
Try to create the mood of a royal banquet in the place where you meet. Ask children to help lay the table and decorate it so that it looks fit for a king or queen. If you're using white paper to cover the table instead of a cloth, children can decorate it with felt tip pens or crayons from the creative corner. Decorate the chairs to make them look grand, by covering with a cloth or pinning a crown to the back.

Put the food on silver foil trays or paper plates along the middle of the table so that children can help themselves easily. If possible, you need enough paper plates to lay a place for everyone around the one big table. Encourage adult helpers to chat with the children while setting up and when sitting down to enjoy the banquet. NB Remember that supportive church members are often happy to help with catering, so make good use of them (bearing in mind food hygiene policies). An appeal in church might produce home-made cakes or conjure up props for the banquet. If you've got somewhere to store some of the royal 'props' used, and have permission to keep them for a few weeks, store them to be reused for another banquet in Session 7.

Picture frames
(5–15 minutes)

If you're going to do 'Masterpieces' later, you will need to do this activity now.

Bible
1 Samuel 16:1–13

Aim
To help children discover that what we're like on the inside is more important to God than how we look. God loves us just as we are, and sees our potential.

Checklist
- Prepare a peaceful atmosphere in the prayer pod.
- Display any pictures from last week's 'Things we fear'.
- Appoint an adult leader to keep an eye on any child who comes to use the pod and to chat or pray with them as necessary.

2

World of a child

This is a vital message for children to grasp in a world where low self-esteem is so common. We don't have to take it to heart when people say unkind things to us, because we know how special we are to God. In leading *Target Challenge,* leaders have the opportunity to demonstrate God's value for individual children by the way we care for each child in the club. This story also touches on what it's like to be the youngest in the family. Bear this in mind when talking with children about their experience of life.

What you need
- Card/sugar paper picture frames made using the template from page 77 and sprayed gold or silver (one each)
- Art and craft materials
- Aprons – if using messy things like glitter glue or paint

What you do
Give each child a picture frame and provide a good selection of art and craft materials. Ask the children to decorate the frames to look really smart because they're going to frame something special. Put each child's name on the back of their frame.

⊙ Picture frames were a brilliant success. The more gaudy the better! We had fun getting very messy. The only disappointment was that the frames were still too wet to use at the end of the session – so the kids couldn't frame their self-portraits. ⊙
Vickie

 Dart ball
(up to 25 minutes)

See Session 1 for instructions and page 16 for ideas for additional games.

4 Hopscotch
(up to 25 minutes)

What you need
- Masking tape to mark out the hopscotch grid on the floor (indoors) or chubby chalk to draw a grid outside if you have a safe outdoor space you can use
- A beanbag or pebble to throw

What you do
Ask some of the children to help you mark out the grid and fill in the numbers. Take it in turns to have a go. Is it difficult getting the beanbag or pebble to land on the right square each time?

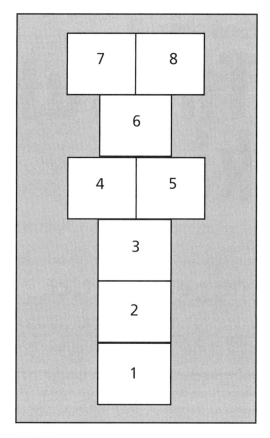

5 Being still exercise
(2–5 minutes)

This is to draw the children together and calm them down at the end of 'Target practice', and to give them a taste of stillness and peace. Note, we're not asking them to empty their minds.

What you need
- CD of calming instrumental music; CD player
- Rugs/mats

What you do
Ask the children to find a space on the floor (preferably on a carpeted area, rug or blanket) and to lie down on their backs for 'Being still'. It's best if the adults get down on the children's level and join in too. You may begin in the same way as for Session 1, if it seemed effective. Ask people to recall last week's Learn and remember verse (Psalm 17:8) and instead of imagining being on a cloud they can picture themselves as little chicks snuggling up to their mother hen, safe under her wing where it's warm and comfortable and they are protected from the cold wind and rain.

Alternatively, you could play 'Sleeping lions' (see Session 1).

At the end, ask them to sit together where they can see the television/projector screen for 'Finding focus'.

Finding focus

◖1 David is chosen
10–15 minutes

What you need
- Dressing up clothes (see text below)
- Multiple choice quiz on flip chart, OHP, or one per child
- DVD and player (if using)

What you do
Begin with a quick recap of the story so far. Last week the children were introduced to a boy called David who worked as a shepherd, defending his dad's (Jesse's) sheep from wild animals, and also enjoyed playing his harp and making up songs in praise of God. He even played his music for King Saul, but his soldier brothers didn't think much of him…

For the next part of the story, dress up one of the children as a prophet with a cape and a staff. Read the following introduction as animatedly as you can:

It's a long day when you work on a farm. Farmers are up at the crack of dawn, and busy with the animals all through the day. Sometimes they are busy most of the night too, when it's lambing time! But it's great when someone comes to visit. That's always a good reason to stop work for a bit, and hear the latest news from the world outside. It might be someone delivering feed for the animals, or perhaps a customer who's come to buy fresh eggs or a sack of potatoes.

Now, Samuel was a prophet, which means he was a messenger of God. And when *he* came visiting, it wasn't just to have a cup of tea and a chat or to buy a dozen eggs! When Samuel came to town, it meant something was up. People would say to each other, 'It's Samuel, the prophet! He must have a message for us from God! What has he come to say? Does this mean God is angry with us? Have we done something wrong? Oh dear, oh dear, oh dear…'

One day, God told Samuel to visit the house of Farmer Jesse. He was on a very important mission, to find a new king! But God's new king turned out to be the *last* person anyone expected!

Show the DVD
(If you are not using the DVD tell the story from the point of view of Eliab, the oldest brother, who was fearful when he heard that the prophet Samuel had arrived, was amazed that he came to their home, was sure he was going to be chosen (after all he was tall and handsome and the oldest and most experienced), was astounded when all his brothers were rejected and angry when David was chosen.)

Read the Bible passage
Photocopy as many copies as you require of the Bible passage on page 70 and read it together. Make sure the multiple choice quiz (on page 28) is visible on an OHP, flip chart or handout. Invite the children to listen carefully to the whole story before doing the quiz.

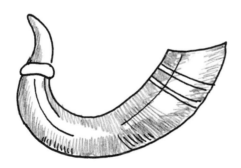

2

Multiple choice quiz

1 What animal did the prophet Samuel take with him for a sacrifice?
a) A calf
b) A lamb
c) A pigeon
d) A duck

2 What did Samuel take to pour on the future king's head?
a) Water
b) Baked beans
c) Sunflower oil
d) Olive oil

3 Which tall, handsome brother did Samuel think God *ought* to choose?
a) David, the youngest
b) Eliab, the oldest
c) Abinadab, a soldier
d) Shammah, in the king's army

4 Why did God choose *David* out of all the brothers?
a) Because God likes shepherds best
b) Because David was really good-looking
c) Because he was strong and a good fighter
d) Because God knew what he was like on the inside

Answers:

1 a) A calf
This is an opportunity to explain what a sacrifice was – a way of giving thanks to God, as well as sometimes being used to take away people's guilt, for a short while, about the bad things they'd done. On this occasion it was probably as a means of praising God, a way of giving God a present.

2 d) Olive oil
You might want to talk about 'anointing' here. Putting oil on someone's forehead was a way of showing that they had been chosen and set apart for a special task, or special attention. In this case it showed that God had chosen David to be the next king, instead of Saul or one of his sons. When Elizabeth II was crowned queen she was anointed with oil in the ceremony.

3 b) Eliab, the oldest

4 d) Because God knew what he was like on the inside

Hitting the spot

You may want to split into smaller groups for some of these activities.

⊙1 Signatures
(5–10 minutes)

What you need
- One photocopy per child of the Signatures list of physical characteristics and sporting achievements, see below. Adapt this chart according to the abilities, characteristics and age of the children in the club.
- A pot of pencils – enough for one each

What you do
Hand out the Signatures lists and pencils. Children can work individually or in pairs. Younger children will need to be paired up with an adult or older child. Explain that, working through the list, they need to find someone who fits each description and ask them for their signature. They write their name next to the characteristic that describes them. For example, they may need to find a very tall person, or someone with green eyes. If you are following on from *Champion's Challenge*, include more questions on sporting achievements. When they've all finished, talk about how, like Samuel, we often judge people by what they look like or by what they have achieved, including sporting success. How do we choose our friends? What's important to us? Are the same things important to God?

Physical characteristics	Signatures
brown eyes	
ginger hair	
blue eyes	
spiky hair	
curly hair	
wears glasses	
pierced ears	
rides a bike without stabilisers	
knocked over all the skittles in one go	
can get a ball through the netball hoop	
scored a goal in football this year	
can swim a width/length	
plays for a school team	
can touch their toes ten times	
can stand on their hands	
can do a somersault	

2

 Masterpieces
(15–30 minutes)

Do this activity in the creative corner.

What you need
- Paints/pencils/pens and A4 paper
- Mirrors
- Decorated picture frames made earlier

What you do
Encourage the children to look in the mirrors and think about how they see themselves, and then draw or paint a self-portrait. When they've finished, ask them what they were thinking as they drew. Are there things that they like/dislike about their appearance? Talk about how God judges people by what's in their hearts. He looks at the inside not the outside. It doesn't matter whether we're big or small, fat or thin, blonde, brunette or ginger – he loves us all the same. He sees us all as *his* masterpieces and he *values* us. That's why we've got our very special frames to put around our self-portraits. Make sure you label each picture and frame with the correct name, keeping them to display in the prayer pod next week.

Learn and remember verse
(5–15 minutes)

What you need
- A large STOP sign
- A mirror/mirrors, or some of the 'Masterpieces' self-portraits
- Poster/OHP of 1 Samuel 16:7 – 'People judge others by what they look like, but I judge people by what is in their hearts.'
- Small copies of the Learn and remember verse on page 66 for the children to take home

What you do
Gather all the children in the prayer pod, reminding them that when they see the STOP sign it means it's time to sit down together. Talk about what the children discovered through doing 'Signatures' and 'Masterpieces'. Explain that what we're like on the inside is more important to God than how we look. God loves us just as we are, and sees our potential with all the gifts and abilities we were born with and the great things we can do with our lives. He knew that young David would make an excellent king one day. We don't have to take it to heart when people say unkind things to us, because we know how special we are to God. Sit in a large circle and repeat the Learn and remember verse several times, reading it once and then reading it all together several times as you pass the mirror round the group. Each child takes a turn at looking into it. Don't forget to include the reference with the memory verse each time.

If you're going to pray, explain how STOP can help us talk with God. You can also incorporate this week's themes:
Sorry (for things we've done that hurt or upset other people, perhaps we've been unkind about how they look)
Thank you (for loving us just as we are and seeing our potential, all that we can be!)
Others (do we know people who are sometimes bullied or feel sad and lonely? Pray that God will show them that he loves them)
Please (help us to be good friends to all sorts of people, not judging by what they look like)
Amen! (Everyone can join in with a loud Amen together at the end.)

Make sure that you say goodbye to each child individually and, if possible talk, with the person who has come to collect each child.

'People judge others by what they look like, but I judge people by what is in their hearts.'

1 Samuel 16:7

3

Session 3
The giant

Bible
1 Samuel
17:4–11,32–37,40–51

Aim
To explore further the idea that God is with us to keep us safe. David knew that he could trust God. He knew that God was stronger and greater than anyone or anything.

When we trust him we can overcome big difficulties.

Checklist
- Prepare the prayer pod to create a calm atmosphere.
- Display children's framed 'Masterpieces' from last week in the prayer pod.
- Appoint an adult leader to keep an eye on any child coming to use the prayer pod. They may want to chat or pray.

Target practice

Welcome the children to *Target Challenge* and give them their badges or name stickers. Welcome any newcomers. If there are several newcomers you may want to make badges again (see Session 1 for details), or just give them a name sticker. Make sure anyone who has had a birthday is made to feel special.

1 Snack – army canteen
(10–20 minutes)

What you need
- A long table for serving food
- Trays for children to collect their food, canteen style
- Army green/camouflage garments/green netting draped around to help set the scene
- Functional looking metal containers/camping plates/bowls/cups (nothing too pretty!)
- 'Chunky' food – nothing too dainty! It might be fun to have something different (beans on toast or dollops of rice pudding in small bowls). Remember to scale down quantities if your club runs after the evening meal
- Drinks

What you do
Set the scene to create the mood of the canteen at an army camp. Ask children to help set up. Encourage adult helpers to chat with the children while setting up and when sitting down (on the floor) to eat.

> *Our group queued up in a very straight line for their beans on toast. We were able to continue the military theme throughout the session, referring to the group as soldiers. It worked really well.*
> *Mary*

2 Dart ball
(up to 25 minutes)

See Session 1. Don't forget to record a score for each child. Is their aim improving? Ideas for additional games are on page 16.

3 Cardboard armour
(up to 25 minutes)

If you're not going to do this exercise, you will need to bring plastic or ready-made cardboard armour for dressing up Goliath.

What you need
- Plenty of cardboard – dismantled grocery boxes?
- String; sticky tape; Blu-tack; scissors; hole puncher
- Kitchen foil to cover the blade of the sword and make it shiny
- A picture of some ancient armour

What you do
Work together with the children to build a set of cardboard armour, including helmet, breastplate, sword, spear, dagger and shield, big enough for a child to wear.

4 Catapults (large or small)
(up to 15 minutes)

What you need

Small version	Large version
Elastic bands	Upturned table
Tissue paper balls	Bungee rope
Tape measure or target	Soft ball or cuddly toy

What you do
Show the children how the catapults work. Be aware of safety issues! Give everyone a go who wants one, making sure they only aim at the

target. See whose paper ball/sponge ball/soft toy goes the furthest, or who can hit a target.

5 Being still exercise
(2–5 minutes)

This will draw the children together and calm them down at the end of 'Target practice'.

What you need
- CD of calming instrumental music; CD player
- Rugs/mats

What you do
Ask the children to find a space on the floor (preferably on a carpeted area, rug or blanket) to lie on their backs for a relaxation exercise. By now they'll know what kind of thing to expect. Start the children off thinking about their bodies, working up from the toes:
scrunch toes up, then let them go (3x)
squeeze knees together, then let them go (3x)
make hands into fists, then shake them out (3x)
shrug shoulders, then drop them (3x)
turn head from side to side (3x)

Then say: 'Close your eyes and imagine you're standing in a big crowd of people waiting to catch a glimpse of someone very special who's going to arrive. Think about how you feel with lots and lots of people all around. What's it like? Hot and smelly? Exciting? A bit worrying? Who are you hoping to see? A king, perhaps? Finally the crowd starts cheering. The Very Important Person has arrived, and you can just about see him through people's legs. But he's not just waving as he drives by. It looks like he's looking for someone specific. He jumps out of his car and starts walking through the crowd towards you. He gets so close you can see his feet! Then he says to the person standing in front of you, "Excuse me, but I'd really like to meet..." (*Tell the children to fill in their own names here, or in a small group, mention all their names.*)

Wow! He's treating YOU like a Very Important Person! How does that make you feel? Remember that feeling while you listen to last week's memory verse: 'People judge others by what they look like, but I judge people by what is in their hearts' (1 Samuel 16:7). God knows you through and through, and he **loves** you.

Alternatively, you could play 'Sleeping lions'. At the end, ask everyone to sit together where they can see the screen for 'Finding focus'.

Finding focus

1 David and Goliath
(10–15 minutes)

What you need
- Pretend armour (plastic, or made earlier)
- DVD and player (if using)
- Space for the game

Dress up one of the older children as Goliath, with all his armour (breastplate, sword, helmet, spear, shield made earlier). Explain that later on they will be finding out what it feels like to fight a fully-armed soldier 'giant' with just a shepherd's crook, sling and five pebbles and wearing **no armour**. Would they think that a young shepherd like David would have any chance of winning the fight?

If you are following on from *Champion's Challenge*, you could talk about any judo or boxing that the children have seen on television. What sort of fighting was this? Have any children ever done any 'fighting' like that? Then introduce Goliath and David as above.

Read the following introduction as animatedly as you can:

They reckon that looking after sheep is quite good practice for looking after people. It teaches you patience, for one thing. Saul had been a shepherd himself, like David. Saul was now the great and mighty king of the people. At first, Saul had been a good leader, but as time went by, he thought more and more about being a king, and less and less about obeying God.

That's why God sent Samuel to choose a new king, David. But even though David trusted God, it didn't really make much sense to him. God's new king? What did it all mean?

Show the DVD
(If you are not using the DVD tell the story using the retold version *The secret weapon*, on pages 38–39 from *The 10 Must know stories* by Heather Butler, in the series of *Must know* books for several age groups which retell the ten Bible stories voted as those that MUST be passed onto the next generation.)

Read the Bible passage
Put the home-made/plastic armour near the four walls (sword one end of the room, spear opposite, helmet and shield on facing walls) Read the Bible passage on page 71, emphasising the highlighted words and as you do so, the

World of a child
This story will be so familiar to you and maybe even some of the children. Familiarity may mean that we fail to realise just how courageous and defiant David was.

Many children have lots of hidden fears. They need to know that God is able to defeat these fears, although not necessarily to make everything come right again by waving a magic wand!

3

children need to listen out for the words 'sword, helmet, spear and shield' – and run to the appropriate wall when they hear them. (This is like the game 'Lifeboats' with 'port, starboard, stern and bow').

Get back together to recap the story with the photocopied passage in front of each child in the group. What happened when David faced Goliath? Key points to draw out:

- Goliath would have killed many soldiers so it was better that David should fight him one-to-one than lots of people fight and be killed.
- Goliath had insulted (said terrible things about) God and that was wrong.
- No one in the Israelite army wanted to fight Goliath – they were too frightened.
- David may not have felt particularly brave or strong; he just wanted to do the right thing, the thing God wanted him to do.
- David knew that God was stronger and greater than anyone or anything. He could trust God to help him and keep him safe, as he had done before.

⊙ We were nervous that tender-hearted children might have been upset about the violence in this story, but in fact they were glad that a 'big, bad bully' got his comeuppance. At 5 years, my daughter was the youngest in the group and did need to talk it through with me afterwards. Was Goliath really dead? Would he come alive again afterwards? Target Challenge felt like a safe place to introduce children to difficult issues such as violence and death in a controlled way. ⊙
Mary

Hitting the spot

(You may want to split into smaller groups for these activities.)

 **Facing Goliath**
(10–20 minutes)

What you need
- A tape measure
- OHP projected image of a soldier, positioned so he looks 9ft (2.74m) tall on the wall, or a cut-out of a 9ft man (alternatively lie three 3ft children on the floor to see how big a 9ft man would look.) We've included an outline of

Goliath on page 78 to blow up on OHP and trace onto 9ft paper
- Something that weighs 15lbs (6.8kg) the same as Goliath's spearhead
- 5 smooth pebbles/rocks
- A sling – use demo model from Session 1

What you do
Show them how big Goliath was, and let them feel the weight of his spearhead. Can they pick it up? Let them hold the five smooth pebbles in their hands and look at the sling again. Can they try to imagine themselves in David's role? Either re-enact it (not using real pebbles!) or talk about it. How would they feel facing a giant soldier with a huge sword and spear, if all they had was five little pebbles and a sling? What would they do? What did David do (trusted God)?

 **Prayer shields**
(10–20minutes)

Do this activity in the prayer pod.

What you need
- Pre-drawn shields for children to cut out of paper
- Pencils/pens

What you do
Introduce this activity with a couple of questions and some discussion. For example, they've thought about how David may have felt, facing Goliath, so do they ever feel like that themselves? Is there something that seems like a really big problem or fear, or an impossible situation that they're facing: bullying, changes, illness, or is someone they know anxious about something like that?

Give each child a shield and a pen, and encourage them to write on their shield a prayer (or draw a picture to represent a prayer; or ask an adult to write for them). Their prayer might be for themselves or for someone else they think might need protection, strength and courage from God at the moment. Would they feel able to pray these prayers aloud? They could do this during the STOP exercise if you're planning to do it. Or could the leader pray a general prayer to cover all of them, and then put them up on the line/pin them on the board and say they'll keep praying for them until something happens?

Look again in weeks to come and see if God has answered in some way. Keep a store of blank shields in the prayer pod with some pencils so that further prayers can be added each week.

 Learn and remember verse
(5–15 minutes)

What you need
- A large STOP sign
- Shield from armour made earlier
- Poster/OHP of Psalm 28:6,7 – 'I praise you, LORD, for answering my prayers. You are my strong shield, and I trust you completely.'
- Small copies of the Learn and remember verse on page 67 for the children to take home

What you do
In the prayer pod, remind them that at *Target Challenge* STOP means sit down. It can also help us to pray. Start with the memory verse. Talk about and demonstrate what a shield is for.

Repeat the memory verse, reading it to them once and then reading it all together several times. Don't forget to include the reference with it.
If you want to pray together, follow the themes of this session:
Sorry (for things we've done that hurt or upset other people)
Thank you (for the good things God has given us)
Others (do we know people who are ill or afraid or need help and protection from God? You can use the children's shield prayers here)
Please (answer my prayers, be my strong shield and help me to trust you)
Amen! (Everyone can join in with a loud Amen together at the end.)

Make sure that you say goodbye to each child individually and if possible talk with the person who has come to collect each child.

Some ideal programmes to use after Target Challenge:

Streetwise

Claire Derry and Julie Sharp

Streetwise is an eight-session midweek club programme that follows the accounts from Luke's Gospel of houses Jesus visited and people Jesus met. It includes games, prayers, stories and discussion. The Streetwise DVD can also be used as part of the programme.

£8.99 978 1 85999 767 3

Awesome!

Sue Clutterham

Together with the *Awesome!* DVD, *Awesome!* helps children explore who Jesus is, using signs from John's Gospel. *Awesome!* is a flexible programme aimed at midweek groups looking to attract non-churched children aged 7 to 11. It has plenty of introductory ideas, ways of presenting the Bible and suggestions for follow-up.

£9.99 978 1 84427 153 5

3

'I praise you, LORD, for answering my prayers. You are my strong shield, and I trust you completely.'

Psalm 28:6,7

Voted the top 10 Bible stories that must be passed onto the next generation, the Must Know Stories is a family of books for all the family.

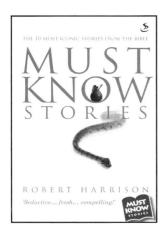

Must Know Stories
Robert Harrison
– told in a compelling, racy style

978 1 84427 320 1
£7.99

The 10 Must Know Stories
Heather Butler
– gripping stories for confident readers

978 1 84427 326 3
£3.99

The Red Book of Must Know Stories
The Green Book of Must Know Stories
Alexander Brown
– five stories in each of these fun books for younger children

Red: 978 1 84427 325 6
Green: 978 1 84427 324 9
£3.99 each

"Once you've been gripped by the Must Know Stories, you'll make sure that everyone you know, whatever their age, must read them too!"

Available from your local Christian bookshop or from Scripture Union Mail Order, PO Box 5148, Milton Keynes MLO MK2 2YX; 0845 0706006; www.scriptureunion.org.uk

All prices correct at the time of going to print

The secret weapon

Question: What sort of things did a shepherd do three thousand years ago?

Answer: He made sure there was grass to munch and water to drink for all his sheep. He protected them from wild animals with his secret weapon, and made sure they didn't get lost. It was an important job but no one, except the sheep themselves, thought shepherds were special.

Question: What was the secret weapon?

Answer: Imagine a strip of leather with a string at each end, like a catapult. The shepherd laid a small stone or pebble on the leather and pulled up the strings. He lifted it up and began spinning, faster and faster and faster. As he released one of the strings, the stone or pebble zipped through the air. Splat! Straight into a fierce, wild animal. This was a shepherd's secret weapon.

Jesse was a farmer and had lots of sons. In fact, he had eight of them. The three oldest were soldiers and they thought they were very important. The youngest was a shepherd and no one except his sheep thought he was important. His name was David. Day after day, he practised killing wild animals using his secret weapon.

David's older brothers, who went by the names of Eliab, Abinadab and Shammah, took themselves off to fight for the Israelite army led by King Saul. The Israelite army was on one side of the Elah Valley. Their enemies, the Philistines, were sprawled out on the other side. Every morning the enemy, in the shape of a whopping sized giant called Goliath, appeared on the opposite hillside and bellowed at the Israelites. Wearing his metal armour, he would swish and swagger through the long grass until he was halfway down the hill.

Then his voice would thunder round the valley. 'Oi, you lot, send your best soldier to fight me! If he kills me, my people will be your slaves. But if I kill him, you Israelites will be our slaves.'

And every morning Saul's army looked at this metal cage on legs. Every morning not a single one of them moved.

In those days, armies didn't provide much for their soldiers. Families had to send their sons food and weapons and anything else they needed. So Jesse, being a farmer, sent a sack of grain and ten loaves of bread to his three sons. He also sent ten large chunks of cheese to their officer to keep him happy. The delivery boy was David.

One day, just as David was dropping off the food, the metal cage on legs lumbered down the opposite hillside.

'What's that?' David asked. He had never seen anything like it.

'Shhh!' his brothers whispered as Goliath hollered rude things about God and the Israelites.

'Who is he?' David breathed. But no one answered him.

They were too scared. Eventually, one soldier whispered that King Saul had said whoever killed Goliath would marry the king's daughter and never have to pay taxes again.

'Wow!

'I'll fight him!' David chirped. 'He doesn't scare me!'

David's brothers tried to shut him up. After all, he was only a shepherd boy. But David kept on and on about it and soon King Saul got to hear. He sent for David.

'But you are only a boy!' Saul sighed. 'Goliath's been a soldier all his life. And he's a giant!'

'So?' David was unimpressed. 'Your majesty, to protect my sheep I chase lions and bears. He's no different and he's making fun of the living God. How dare he? I can kill him. God will keep me safe.'

Saul tapped his fingers on his sword. This was the first offer he'd had. At least this scruffy little kid believed in God.

'Go on then,' he said, 'but you'll wear my armour to keep you safe.' David remained unimpressed. The helmet came over his eyes, the sword made his arm ache and the shield was almost as big as he was.

Perhaps the armour of someone shorter would fit. But even the smallest helmet slid down David's nose, the sword was still too heavy and he still couldn't see over the shield. David made up his mind. He was going onto the battlefield, just himself, his secret weapon and the living God. So there!

A stream babbled down the hillside. David bent over, chose five smooth pebbles, checked they were the right size, and then strode towards Goliath.

Goliath didn't notice David at first. He was not expecting someone so small without any armour. When he spotted him he

howled with laughter. 'When I've finished with you, I'll feed you to the vultures and wolves and bears,' he roared.

David stood his ground and yelled. 'You come to fight me with a sword and a spear and a dagger. But I've come out to fight you in the name of the living God. I'll knock you down and tear off your head. Everybody will see that God doesn't need swords or spears to save his people.'

Question: What do you do if you are small and a giant comes lumbering towards you?

Answer: You load your secret weapon and whizz it round your head. You wait until the giant is close enough so you can see his teeth and hear the leather of his shin pads creaking. Then you release the stone.

Shepherds rarely miss. They practise every day, and as usual, David was deadly accurate. His stone went straight into the middle of the giant's helmet where there was a gap. Goliath needed that gap to be able to see. But from that moment, he didn't see anything ever again.

The Philistine soldiers watched everything. They saw their giant hero lying dead. They ran. The Israelite soldiers watched everything too. They chased after the Philistines. Their feet pounded down the hill. Their lungs gasped as they raced up the other side. They crashed through the tents and weapons and supplies of food the Philistines had left behind. They carried on and won.

After the chase, David came back to the army tents. He was clutching the head of the giant. He was also clutching his secret weapon. He was only a shepherd boy but before long he would be a great king.

Taken from *The 10 Must Know Stories*

4

Session 4
The singer

Bible
1 Samuel 18:6–16

Aim
To explore how music affects our feelings and how we can use it to express our emotions. We can also use music and singing to praise God, as David did, and this is a good thing to do.

Checklist
- Display children's 'Masterpieces' from Session 2 and 'Prayer Shields' from Session 3 in the prayer pod.
- Have an adult leader keep an eye on any child who comes to the prayer pod.
- If using paints or glitter glue, have aprons or old shirts to protect children's clothes.
- If possible, invite a musician to join you this week. Give them plenty of warning and clear instructions as to what you'll need them to do.
- If you have access to tambourines or shakers, bring them along for anyone who doesn't make an elastic band harp.

Target practice

Welcome the children to *Target Challenge*. Make sure everyone has either a name badge or a sticker and that anyone who has had a birthday is made to feel special.

🕐1 Elastic band harps
(2–5 minutes)

What you need
- A collection of small boxes without lids, eg matchboxes, chocolate boxes, small gift/jewellery boxes (you may need to put out a plea to all church members to get enough for every child)
- Lots of elastic bands of different thickness/size, to fit snugly over the boxes
- Stickers/glue/things for decorating the 'harps'

What you do
Each child needs to 'string' their box with 3–5 elastic bands to make a slightly different 'note' when plucked.

🗣 The children loved making their elastic band harps and felt a real sense of achievement. We made a point of all playing them together sitting on the mat before 'Being still'. 🗣
Vickie

🕐2 Snack – jazz cafe
(10–30 minutes)

What you need
- Small tables and chairs
- Checked tablecloths (cafe style)
- A blackboard with a menu on it
- Plates, cups and serviettes
- Food – use whatever you like (eg little sandwiches, crisps, fruit, cake) but plate it up

in advance, with a little bit of everything on each plate. Use some sort of 'garnish' to make each plateful look special! Remember to scale down the food element if the club is after the evening meal, and always check for food allergies!
- Drinks
- Background music – either a recording, or, even better, a live performance! Is there someone on the team or in your church worship group who would be able or willing to join you for this session to play keyboard/saxophone/clarinet jazz-style throughout 'Target practice', to demonstrate some different kinds of music in 'Finding focus' and to teach a simple song later on?

What you do
Set the scene to create the mood of a jazz cafe. Dim the lights. Use table lamps on tables (if it's safe to do so). Ask a few children to help as waiters or waitresses, bringing plates of food to children seated at the tables. Encourage adult helpers to pull up a chair to chat with the children while everyone is being served. If you have live music, don't forget to listen and clap at the end! The children won't be able to help feeling that this is a very special occasion.

🕐3 Dart ball
(up to 25 minutes)

See Session 1. Don't forget to record a score for each child. Is their aim improving? Ideas for additional games are on page 16.

🕐4 Skittles
(up to 25 minutes)

What you need
- A set of skittles and two balls (or several sets if you're expecting lots of children)

What you do
See how many skittles each child can knock over with their two balls. Alternatively bring lots of balls and let them keep trying until all the skittles are knocked over. How many tries does it take?

 Being still exercise
(2–5 minutes)

What you need
- Musician, prepared to play different kinds of music
- Or a selection of CDs and a player
- Rugs/mats

What you do
Draw the children together and ask them to find a space on the floor to lie on their backs with their eyes closed. Stick to the musical theme. If you have a musician, prime them to play short bursts of contrasting pieces/speeds/styles of music, while the children listen. Tell the children to think about how each piece makes them feel. If you don't have a musician, bring a compilation of different kinds of music and play snatches for the children. Ask the children to talk about how the different kinds of music made them feel – happy, sad, excited, frightened? If appropriate, play the theme tune from the Olympics or the tune from the *Champion's Challenge* holiday club.

Points to draw out: music affects our emotions. A skilled musician can play music that soothes people who are ill or troubled, or music to help others sing praises to God. If we make up our own songs we can express our feelings in the music, just as David did in the songs (psalms) that he wrote.

Finding focus

 David the musician
(10–15 minutes)

What you need
- Musician, prepared to play different kinds of music
- Home-made harps (if you have them)
- DVD and player (if using)
Your musician (if you have one) is your visual (and audio) aid. Read the following introduction as animatedly as you can:

Goliath was dead. The mighty warrior, champion of the Philistine army, nine feet tall and built like a tank, had been beaten by a young shepherd boy. All those hours David had spent practising with the sling had certainly paid off! And as he marched home with the soldiers of King Saul, David was about to find that his skill at playing the harp would come in pretty handy, too.

Show the DVD
(If you are not using the DVD, move straight on to reading the Bible passage interactively.)

Read the Bible passage
Photocopy the Bible passage on page 72 as required. Read together with your musician playing a suitable accompaniment.
Paragraphs 1 and 2: happy, dancing music
Paragraphs 3 and 4: angry music
Paragraph 5: 'Saul was afraid' music (Jaws theme?) **or** 'God looked after David, happy music' again
Children can join in with their 'harps' at the appropriate moment. Tell them to listen out for the words 'tambourine' and 'harp' and play along with the musician when they hear them.

Some points to bring out in discussion:
- The women were singing to praise King Saul and David for winning the battle with the Philistines.
- It made Saul jealous and angry that David got so much attention. He thought that all the praise ought to go to him, the king.
- When Saul lost his temper, David thought that playing the harp might help calm him down, but this time it didn't work, and Saul threw his spear at David.
- Saul sent David out to fight in the army because he hoped David would get killed in battle.
- The Lord God helped David, so he, with the soldiers he led, kept winning their battles.

World of a child
Children enjoy making music just as they enjoy writing poetry. Both activities are an important part of the curriculum in school. Encourage their creativity.

Remember that you do not want to put words of worship of God into the mouths of children who do not know him and therefore are not yet able to worship him. This is a very important point to hold on to if you are seeking to reach out to children on or beyond the fringe of church. Choose songs that say important truths about God, yet do not assume any commitment to him.

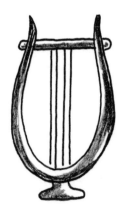

4

Hitting the spot

You may want to split into smaller groups for these activities

⊙1 A Target Challenge Psalm
(5–20 minutes)

What you need
- Flip chart/OHP and suitable pens
- Some copies of Psalm 18:1–3 for older children to look at

What you do
Explain that David was so talented at playing the harp that he became the royal musician. This wasn't always easy because Saul was very jealous and bad-tempered at times, as we've heard. However, David also used his music to express his feelings, being happy, sad or frightened. He wrote lots of songs and poems to praise God for being so great. Because David knew God helped him, he used his music to thank God for his help, too. Listen to one of these songs, Psalm 18:1–3. You can imagine David singing it to the Lord after the Lord had rescued him from his enemies, especially Saul!

'I love you, LORD God, and you make me strong.
You are my mighty rock, my fortress, my protector,
the rock where I am safe, my shield,
my powerful weapon, and my place of shelter.
I praise you, LORD!
I prayed, and you rescued me from my enemies.'

Encourage the children to have a go at writing their own psalm. Ask them: 'How are you all feeling today? What do you want to tell God about? Do you want to ask him for his help? Or has he answered one of your prayers and you want to thank him? You could look at last week's shield prayers for inspiration. David thinks of God being like a castle or a piece of armour or a shelter. How else could you describe God? God loves to listen to our thoughts and feelings.'

Put everyone's ideas together and try to write your own *Target Challenge* psalm.

Recognise that some children will not be sure what it means to talk with God. Offer to help any children for whom this is the case. You could take as a model the first verses of Psalm 24 which says more about God's creation rather than God himself. For some children this will be

a bridge from their world into an understanding of who God is.

The children's songs will be quite rough round the edges. Don't worry. It doesn't have to rhyme or scan, or be set to music, although you could attempt this with an older group if you choose a very simple tune everyone knows. Alternatively, children are used to composing music using instruments at school. A group of children could work with your live musician or use body percussion or actual instruments to create music which reflects what they want to say to God.

This activity is simply an expression of the children's emotions and where they are in their spiritual journey. Leaders may need to inject ideas to get the children started.

⊙2 A Target Challenge psalm picture
(5–10 minutes)

What you need
- Tissue paper; scissors and glue
- A3 sheets of paper

What you do
Talk about how music paints pictures in our imaginations. Psalm 18 or 24 give us lots of things to imagine. Ask the children to think of one image from either psalm and then recreate it using glue and tissue paper. You could use other media such as paint, felt-tip pens, crayons or coloured material.

⊙3 Song of Praise
(5–10 minutes)

What you need
- Either your musician with his/her instrument; music; words on OHP/flip chart or handouts
- Or a CD, tape/DVD with children's songs (and player)

What you do
Teach the children a simple song that's based on a psalm that says something about God without putting words into the children's mouths that they cannot mean. Or if you've already learnt one together in previous weeks, remind them of how it goes. You can tell the children that this is the kind of song David wrote about God. Christians still use David's psalms to praise God today!

⊙4 Learn and remember verse
(5–15 minutes)

What you need
- A large STOP sign
- Tambourines, shakers (including bunches of keys), elastic band harps from earlier
- Poster/OHP of Psalm 147:1 – 'Shout **praises** to the LORD! Our God is kind, and it is right and good to sing **praises** to him.'
- Small copies of the Learn and remember verse on page 67 for the children to take home

What you do
Gather all the children to pray together in the prayer pod. Repeat the Learn and remember verse several times, reading it to them once and then reading it all together. Whenever you read the word 'praises' pause to shake shakers/twang harps etc. Don't forget to include the reference with the Learn and remember verse each time. If you want to, you could read your *Target Challenge* psalm or sing your song of praise once again at the end, as praise to God, or you could make up some 'shouts of praise' to finish. Ask the children what they have learned about God so far at *Target Challenge*. They could shout praise to him for his protection, his love, because he is kind and good, or because he can always be trusted.

If helpful, use STOP to help you close in prayer, incorporating this week's theme.

Sorry (for things we've done that hurt other people, like Saul throwing his spear at David)

Thank you (for the good things God has given us – you could use your 'shouts of praise' here)

Others (you may have some more 'shield prayers' to use here)

Please (teach me how to sing your praises, like David did)

Amen! (Everyone can join in with a loud Amen together at the end.)

Make sure that you say goodbye to each child individually and, if possible, talk with the person who has come to collect each child.

Some ideal programmes to use after Target Challenge:

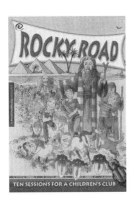

Rocky Road

Rosey King

A ten-session programme for leaders running a midweek club for children, based on the story of Moses. *Rocky Road* includes gripping storytelling ideas, imaginative crafts and relationship-building opportunities. Can be used as a follow-up programme to a *Pyramid Rock* holiday club.

£9.99 978 1 84427 183 2

Clues2Use

Jean Elliott

Join the Landlubbers pirates as they follow clues to discover Jesus in the 21st century! Using the *Jesus Quest* DVD, this eight-session midweek club programme helps children see how Jesus is always with them. Can be used as a follow-up programme to a *Landlubbers* holiday club. The *Jesus Quest DVD* is alos available from www.agape.org.uk

£9.99 978 1 84427 113 9

4

'Shout **praises** to the LORD! Our God is kind, and it is right and good to sing **praises** to him.'

Psalm 147:1

Session 5
The friends

Target practice

Welcome the children to *Target Challenge*.
Make sure everyone has either a name badge or
a sticker and ensure anyone who has had a
birthday is made to feel special.

Snack – Friends' cafe
(10–30 minutes)

What you need
- Picnic rugs and scatter cushions with a low coffee table
- Paper plates, cups and serviettes if needed
- Finger food (eg little sandwiches, crisps, fruit and cake). Remember to scale down the food element if the club is just before or after the evening meal.
- Drinks – hot chocolate 'cappuccino' (with frothed milk and a sprinkle of chocolate)
- Background music
- A blackboard with a 'menu' on it

What you do
Make hot chocolate early and allow it to cool
before serving (or it takes too long to drink).
Note that frothed milk and sprinkled topping
need to be added at the last minute for best
effect. Try to create the mood of an informal
café in the place where you meet. Dim the lights
to soften the atmosphere. Encourage adult
helpers to chat with the children whilst
everyone is eating. It would be good to start
talking about friends – who their friends are,
what they like to do together, in preparation for
the session's theme.

Dart ball
(up to 25 minutes)

See Session 1. Don't forget to record a score for
each child. Is their aim improving? Additional
ideas for games are on page 16.

Cotton bud javelins
(up to 10 minutes)

What you need
- Drinking straws (wide ones)
- Cotton buds (not too chunky)
- Tape measure or target

What you do
Show children how to blow a cotton bud
through a straw. You must warn them not to
suck and not to aim towards other people.
Give everyone a go that wants one, but one at a
time. See whose cotton bud javelin goes the
furthest, or who can hit a target.

4 Fantastic friends
(10 minutes)

What you need
- Paper
- Art and craft materials
- Aprons or old shirts if using paint

What you do
Encourage the children to draw or paint pictures
of what they like to do with their friends. Whilst
they're drawing, chat with individuals about
their friends, and about what they're drawing.
Other topics you might raise: how do you
choose your friends? What's the most important
thing about a friend? How do we show our
friends that we care for them, that they're
important to us? You might want to come
together in the prayer pod afterwards to look at
their pictures. Talk about these things as a
group, before moving on to the next activity.

*Our group was so calm and
relaxed after 'Fantastic friends' and
we'd spent so much time talking
about friendship that we decided to
skip the 'Being still' exercise and
move straight on to 'Finding focus'.*
Mary

Bible
1 Samuel 20:1–3,
12,13,17–23,35–42

Aim
To explore the
friendship between
David and Jonathan and
to help children think
about what makes a
true friend.

How, in practical ways,
can we show our
friends that we care? To
introduce children to
the idea of praying for
friends as another way
of helping them.

Checklist
- Prepare the prayer pod. You could display last week's *Target Challenge* psalm and Learn and remember verse.
- An adult leader will need to keep an eye on any child who comes to use the pod.
- If using paints or glitter glue, make sure you have aprons or old shirts to protect children's clothes, especially school uniform!
- Photocopy the Bible script so that children can read it to the rest of the group.

5

World of a child

Friendship is so important to children – falling out, having a best friend, being left out of the gang! Some children will find making friends very difficult. Encourage the children to talk about this with you and with God, who is the best friend ever.

⏱5 Being still exercise
(2–5 minutes)

What you need
- CD of instrumental music to play in background; CD player
- Rugs/mats

What you do
To draw the children together and calm them down so they can focus at the end of 'Target practice', ask them to find a space on the floor to lie on their backs with their eyes closed for the 'being still' exercise. This could involve consciously tensing and relaxing neck, shoulders, arms, hands, fingers, legs, feet, toes. They might also concentrate on breathing in and out slowly. Last week's Learn and remember verse was about praising God (Psalm 147:1). Can you use that in some way? Suggest that the children imagine that they're playing outside somewhere with their best friends. Ask them: Where are you? What are you doing? How do you feel?

Alternatively, you could play 'Sleeping lions'.

Finding focus

▶1 David's friends
(10–15 minutes)

What you need
- DVD and player (if using)

Read the following introduction as animatedly as you can:

Well, it was quite a change for David, as you can imagine, living at the palace and leading the king's armies in battle. He was used to the farm and the animals and spending hours by himself out in the side pasture, looking after his sheep. Now he was surrounded by kings and princes and courtiers and servants. I should think there were times when David wished he was back with his sheep!

But at least David had one good friend at the palace – and no less a person than the king's own son, Prince Jonathan. And the king even honoured David by giving him the hand of his daughter, the Princess Michal, in marriage. So now the king was his father-in-law and Jonathan was his brother-in-law! Sounds great, eh? But things aren't always as they seem. And David certainly had to stay on his guard…

Show the DVD

(If you are not using the DVD, tell the story as follows, making suitable hand signs which the children can copy. To introduce the story talk about friendship and what best friends do with and for each other (*clasp hands as two people holding hands*):

David and Jonathan were best friends even though Jonathan was King Saul's son and might have been expecting to become king (*place imaginary crown over head*), yet David had been chosen by God to be king (*refer back to Session 2 and pour oil over an imaginary head*). But Saul had turned against David and wanted him dead (*throw imaginary javelin*)! He even sent guards to kill David in his bed. Jonathan told David he might need to escape forever (*hands urging someone to go*). He created a plan. David was to hide in a certain field, beside the Going-away Rock. At a great feast, Jonathan would check out with his father, the king, just how much he wanted David dead. If it was good news, Jonathan would fire three arrows beside David (*shooting arrow movements*). If it was bad news, he would shoot three arrows way beyond where David was hiding (*shoot three more arrows*). It was bad news! David and Jonathan wept (*wipe eyes*) and very sad, David went away.

Read the Bible passage
Photocopy the Bible passage on page 73 and choose three (older) readers to read it out – narrator, David and Jonathan. Three of the children can enact scene 2 while it's being read, playing David, Jonathan and Jonathan's servant. The winner of the cotton bud javelin competition could play Jonathan if their aim is good enough to be safe!

Ask the children what they think happened, using open questions. Aim to bring out the following points:
- Jonathan risked his own life to protect David from King Saul.
- Jonathan and Michal had split loyalty because Saul was their dad, but their consciences told them that the right thing to do was to help their friend.
- David and Jonathan were very sad because they thought they might never see each other again.
- Ask the children: 'Has a friend ever asked you for help? What did you do? Have you ever had a friend move away or leave your school? What did that feel like?' Say how friends are very important to us.

Hitting the spot

⊙1 Musical islands
(10 minutes)

What you need
- CD player and music (with someone to switch it on and off)
- Plenty of large newspaper pages. It is important not to use papers with small pages, since the game would get too difficult too quickly!

What you do
Spread the newspaper sheets on the floor – one each for half the children. Encourage the children to move around the room to the music. When the music stops they have to find a friend and jump on a piece of newspaper together, taking care not to slip. No part of either of them must touch the floor around it. The newspaper should be ripped a bit smaller each time, so it gets harder to do. They may need to carry each other in the end to fit on!

⊙2 Thanks for being my friend bookmark
(10 minutes)

What you need
- Strip of card to make a bookmark with hole punched in the top
- Glitter pens or felt-tip pens
- Glitter wool

What you do
Cut pieces of wool the same length to thread through the hole to make a toggle. The children write on the card a message to someone they want to thank for being their friend.

⊙3 Prayer web
(10–20 minutes)

What you need
- A ball of string

What you do
Ask the children to stand in a circle. Hold the ball of string, with the loose end tied round your finger. Explain that everyone needs to think of a friend to pray for; someone who they think is hurting or alone or has been ill. The person who has the ball of string says the name of the friend they want to pray for and then throws the ball of string to someone else. The second person wraps the string loosely around their hand before naming their friend and passing the string. When everyone has prayed for someone there will be a web of string to show how praying for one another brings us closer together. Talk about how David and Jonathan prayed for one another and helped each other, which showed what true, loyal friends they were. Praying for a friend is another way of helping them and showing you care.

⊙4 Learn and remember verse
(5–15 minutes)

What you need
- A large STOP sign
- Your pictures of 'Fantastic friends'
- Poster/OHP of Proverbs 18:24 (NIV, not CEV) – 'There is a friend who sticks closer than a brother.'
- Small copies of the Learn and remember verse, on page 68 for the children to take home

What you do
In the prayer pod, look at the 'Fantastic friends' pictures again. Remind the children that we've talked about what makes a good friend, and how we can help others and show we care, as Jonathan helped David. Ask them if they know that God says we can be *his* friends, too, and if we are, he promises he'll never, ever leave us or let us down? He's a true friend, and sticks closer than a brother. Repeat the Learn and remember verse several times, reading it to them once and then reading it all together. Don't forget to include the reference each time to remind the children that this is a verse from the Bible. Remind the children that STOP can help us to pray.
Sorry (for things we've done that hurt or upset other people)
Thank you (for the good things God has given us, like friends!)
Others (you could use the 'Prayer web' exercise here, if you didn't do it earlier)
Please (be my friend, and help me to be a good friend to others)
Amen!
Make sure that you say goodbye to each child individually and, if possible, talk with the person who has come to collect each child.

5

'There is a friend who sticks closer than a brother.'

Proverbs 18:24

Session 6
The outlaw

Target practice

Welcome the children to *Target Challenge*. Make sure everyone has either a name badge or a sticker and ensure anyone who has had a birthday is made to feel special.

 Craft campfire
(5–30 minutes)

You will need to do this if you're having a campfire supper for your snack and are not going outside.

What you need
- Some large stones or big scrunched up bits of grey paper to look like stones
- Dry logs/sticks or cardboard
- Art and craft materials including felt-tip pens, Sellotape/Blu-tack and scissors
- Tissue paper or coloured foil paper (red, orange, yellow)
- A torch with good batteries
What you <u>won't</u> need: matches!!

What you do
Place the stones in a circle for a fireplace. If you have real logs/sticks, arrange them in a wigwam shape, leaving a gap in the middle for the torch. If not, colour some cardboard to look like wood and roll it up to make logs, then arrange like a campfire, again with a space in the middle for the torch. Crumple up some large red pieces of tissue paper and tuck them into the heart of the 'fire'. Cut out flame shapes from the orange and yellow pieces of tissue paper and attach them to logs. Finally, switch on the torch and put it in the middle of the fire for the full, glowing effect.

Note: You will need to sit around this campfire for your meal, so build it where you need it. (It won't be easy to move!) If you've got somewhere to store the logs, stones and tissue paper you used for this activity, keep hold of them for Session 8, when the fire is recreated for visiting parents/carers.

2 Snack – Campfire supper
(10–30 minutes)

What you need
- Picnic rugs and blankets/shawls to wrap round people's shoulders
- Paper or plastic plates, cups
- Campfire food (hot dogs, toast and baked beans). Remember to scale down the food element if club is after a mealtime
- Drinks
- Craft campfire

What you do
Set the scene to create the mood of an open-air camp. Dim the lights so the campfire glow is the focus of attention. Encourage children to put shawls, scarves or travel rugs round their shoulders and to sit round the 'fire' on the ground, as if sitting outside on a chilly evening. Encourage adult helpers to chat with the children while everyone is eating.

Note: The campfire element might suggest to you the possibility of a family event around a campfire with food, music and games. The time of year will affect the suitability of this. You might even consider going outside for this session and having a real campfire!

3 Dart ball
(up to 25 minutes)
See Session 1. Don't forget to record a score for each child. Is their aim improving? Additional games are on page 16.

Bible
1 Samuel 24:1–11,16–20

Aims
To explore how jealousy spoils relationships (Saul wanted to murder David).

To consider David's response when presented with the opportunity to 'get his own back' (he could have killed Saul).

To show that God was with David, even when everything seemed to be going wrong – and he's with us all the time, too.

Checklist
- Display the 'Fantastic friends' pictures from last session in the prayer pod.
- An adult leader will need to keep an eye on any child who comes to use the prayer pod.
- If using paints or glitter glue, make sure you have aprons or old shirts to protect children's clothes,

6

World of a child
The children are not likely to experience someone plotting to kill them but they know about jealousy, both from the angle of being jealous themselves and experiencing the consequences of jealous behaviour. Pray that in this session you will have opportunities to explore their responses and to see that God is with us when we feel we are wronged.

⊕4 Pin the tail on the sheep
(up to 10 minutes)

What you need
- A large drawing of a sheep (without a tail)
- A cardboard cut-out lamb's tail with Blu-tack on the back
- Pencil to mark an X and children's initials
- Blindfold

What you do
Give each child a go at sticking the tail on the sheep, blindfold, and see who gets closest to the right spot.

⊕5 Being still exercise
(2–5 minutes)

What you need
- CD of instrumental music to play in background; CD player
- Rugs/mats

What you do
To draw the children together and help them focus at the end of 'Target practice', ask them to find a space on the floor and to lie down on their backs with eyes closed for a relaxation exercise. This could involve consciously tensing and relaxing neck, shoulders, arms, hands, fingers, legs, feet, toes. They might also concentrate on breathing in and out slowly.

Say to the children: 'Now, can you imagine that you're David and you've run away from Saul? You're hiding in a deep, dark cave (think about what that would feel like: cold, damp, scary, lonely?) and you're wondering how you're ever going to become king (have you got any ideas how that might happen?)… Last session's Learn and remember verse said that 'There is a friend that sticks closer than a brother' (Proverbs 18:24). Jonathan was a true friend to you, and helped you to escape from King Saul, when he threatened to kill you. But you have another very special friend whom you trust completely: God.

In one of David's songs of praise to God he talked about how he felt the Lord was always near, to comfort and protect him. Now listen to the words of the psalm and think about whether knowing God is very close by can make you feel less scared, less lonely and more confident, because he sees into your heart and he loves you.'

Psalm 139:1–5
You have looked deep
into my heart, Lord,
and you know all about me.
You know when I am resting
or when I am working,
and from heaven
you discover my thoughts.
You notice everything I do
and everywhere I go.
Before I even speak a word,
you know what I will say,
and with your powerful arm
you protect me
from every side.

Alternatively, you could play 'Sleeping lions'.

Finding focus

◑1 David as an outlaw
(15–25 minutes, with quiz)

What you need
- DVD and player (if using)

Read the following introduction as animatedly as you can:
Poor old David. On the run, and a long way from home. A long way from the farm he'd known as a boy. And a far cry from the palace where he'd been royal musician to King Saul. No longer the hero of the people – now he was an outlaw. David was hiding in the mountains with a few friends, loyal soldiers who'd served with him in the army as he won victory after victory. But who was he hiding from? The king. Yes, Saul had finally given up pretending to like David. He couldn't get it out of his mind that David was after his crown. All he could think of now was to kill David.

David wasn't really afraid. He knew that God was with him. One of David's songs, called psalms, says 'The Lord's my shepherd.' He knew that God would keep him safe, even when things looked pretty bad…

Show the DVD
(If you are not using the DVD, move straight onto the Bible passage on page 72 and quiz on page 51–52, checking that the children have understood the story.)

Bible Quiz

1   How many soldiers did Saul bring to capture David?
   a) Thirty
   b) Three hundred
   c) Three thousand

2   Where was David hiding?
   a) In a shepherd's hut
   b) In a cave
   c) In a tent

3   What did David take from Saul without him noticing?
   a) A bit of cloth from his robe
   b) A bit of hair from his head
   c) His sword from his belt

4   What did David do next?
   a) Danced around saying, "Ha ha, I could have killed you and one day I *will*!"
   b) Stayed hiding in the back of the cave until Saul had gone away
   c) Came and bowed down to Saul and said, "I could have killed you but I won't hurt you because you're still God's chosen king."

5   What did Saul say in reply?
   a) "You'll never leave this cave. Now I've found you I'm going to kill you!"
   b) "You're a better person than me – I know you'll be a great king one day!"
   c) "You've never shown me respect and you'll never be king!"

Answers:

1 c) Three thousand

2 b) In a cave

3 a) A bit of cloth from his robe

4 c) Came and bowed down to Saul...

5 b) "You're a better person than me..."

6

Read the Bible passage

What you need
- Quiz questions and answers on page 51, copied onto a flip chart, acetate or printed on slips of paper, one for each pair of children.

What you do
Put the quiz questions up on a flip chart or acetate, or give them out on slips of paper. Read them through, for the benefit of younger children. Tell the children to listen for the answers as you read the Bible passage. Now read the Bible passage in a way that brings out all the drama. With young children you might want to pause at the end of each paragraph to work out the right answers together as you go along. Some points to bring out as you go:
- After question 1, say how jealousy spoils friendships. David had always tried to help Saul, but Saul was too jealous to respond kindly. You could refer back to what you discussed about friendship in the last session.
- After questions 3 and 4, say how David kept God's promises and laws in mind, so he didn't listen to his friends when they told him to kill Saul and seize his chance for power. He knew it would be wrong to do that, and he trusted God to make him king some other way.

When the stones are finished, gather the children in a large circle and explain that whatever's happening, God is with them and loves them. Even when everything seemed to be going wrong, David knew God was with him and he trusted God to sort things out. Ask the children to take it in turns to place their pebble in the centre of the circle to build a cairn. As they put their stone down they can simply say, 'God is with us' or older children might like to pray something personalised, eg 'God is with me when I'm… (worried/happy/sad/lonely etc)'

When the cairn is finished, close the exercise with a prayer or read the verses again from Psalm 139 or Psalm 46:1, the Learn and remember verse. Children can take their pebbles home as a reminder that God is with them, or if you have space in the prayer pod, keep the cairn there as a visual reminder until the final session.

Our stones were spray-painted silver, making them look really special, and I think this added value to the activity. None of the children appeared to be uncomfortable praying this way and leaders took part too. Building the cairn is a good illustration but also a great tool for introducing children to prayer.
Vickie

Hitting the spot

◎1 God-with-us Cairn
(10–25 minutes)

What you need
- Enough large pebbles for one each
- Felt-tip pens for decorating pebbles

What you do
Give each child a pebble to hold. Talk about how piles of stones, called cairns are used to mark paths in wild places like mountains. Maybe that's how David found his way to Wild Goat Rocks. Explain to the children that they're going to decorate their stones, using felt-tip pens, and then build a cairn of their own. As children decorate their stones, encourage leaders to talk with them about what's happening in their lives at the moment. Are things going well? Is there anything they're worried or unhappy about at the moment? Also find out about what the children are happy about. We are not just interested in the struggles of life, neither is God!

◎2 Washing line
(10–15 minutes)

What you need
- A washing line and pegs
- Strips of cloth
- Felt-tip pens or paints

What you do
David was sorry that he had cut off the corner of Saul's robe without Saul noticing. He felt that he had harmed the king, God's chosen leader. He had not trusted God as he should have done. Saul also realised that he could have been killed and was sorry for his jealousy of David. Invite the children to draw on a bit of cloth a symbol of something that reminds them of either a time when they have been jealous or of a time when they have known God to keep them safe and they have trusted him. For example, a bed for when they are asleep or a friend who is good at sports symbolised by a goal mouth.

6

◎3 Learn and remember verse
(5–15 minutes)

What you need
- A large STOP sign
- Poster/OHP of Psalm 46:1 – 'God is our mighty fortress, always ready to help in times of trouble.'
- Small copies of the Learn and remember verse on page 68 for the children to take home

What you do
Gather all the children in the prayer pod and talk to them about castles and fortresses. How were castles built to keep people safe? *(Thick walls, a moat, perhaps built on a hill so they could see the enemy coming from a long way off and be prepared.)* Explain that God is like a fortress, a safe place to go when we're having a tough time (like David was). If we pray to him, he hears us and will help us. Can any of the leaders talk about a time when God was a 'fortress' for them, and how he helped them?

How do the children think God might be able to help *them*? Repeat the Learn and remember verse several times, reading it to them once and then reading it all together. Don't forget to include the reference each time.
Use STOP to help you pray:
Sorry (if we've let jealousy spoil our friendships, or have tried to repay wrong with wrong)
Thank you (that God never leaves us, is always there to help)
Others (does anyone they know need to hear that God can be their fortress?)
Please (help me to trust you and do the right thing, even when I'm having a hard time)
Amen!

Make sure that you say goodbye to each child individually and, if possible, talk with the person who has come to collect each child.

6

'God is our mighty fortress, always ready to help in times of trouble.'

Psalm 46:1

Session 7
King David

Target practice

Welcome the children to *Target Challenge.* Make sure everyone has either a name badge or a sticker and ensure anyone who has had a birthday is made to feel special.

1 Royal icing
(10 minutes)

What you need
- A table to work on, separate from the banqueting table
- Plain biscuits or un-iced fairy cakes (enough for one each)
- Icing/writing icing/cake decorations/sprinkles
- A large 'silver' (or foil covered) serving platter to display the iced cakes/biscuits when finished
- Small squares of clean paper or serviettes and pen for writing children's names on

What you do
Encourage each child to ice/decorate a biscuit or small cake for the banquet. It must be fit for a king!! When the iced cakes are done, display them on the big 'silver' platter on the banqueting table, ready to eat at the end of the meal. (If you want to be sure each child eats their own creation, slip a small square of named paper underneath each cake.)
Note: Remember that supportive church members are often happy to help with catering, so ask them to provide some home-baked plain fairy cakes and biscuits for icing. Bought cakes are usually iced already, so are not ideal for this purpose.

2 Snack – royal banquet
(10–25 minutes)

What you need
- A long table with chairs around it
- A long, dark red or purple tablecloth or a roll of white paper to use as table covering
- Decorations: candlesticks (with unlit candles), flowers/greenery, a large bunch of grapes in a 'silver' (kitchen foil covered) fruit bowl
- Paper plates
- Party finger food: crisps, cocktail sausages, 'Royal icing' creations etc. If it's near a mealtime, scale down the amount of food
- Drinks (eg blackcurrant squash in plastic wine glasses or paper cups decorated by the children)

What you do
Ask children to help lay the table and decorate it so it looks fit for a king or queen. If you're using white paper to cover the table instead of a cloth, children can decorate it with felt-tip pens or crayons from the creative corner. Decorate paper cups in a similar way. Put the savoury food on 'gold/silver' paper plates along the middle of the table so that the children can help themselves easily. You need enough paper plates to lay a place for everyone around the one big table, if possible. Encourage adult helpers to chat with the children while you set up and finally sit down to enjoy your banquet.

3 Dart ball
(up to 15 minutes)

See Session 1. Don't forget to record a score for each child. Is their aim improving? Alternative games suggestions are on pages 16 and 17.

Bible
2 Samuel
5:1–4,17–20; 6:1–5

Aim
To show that God keeps his promises just as he kept his promise to David that he would become king. David's response was to celebrate with singing and dancing.

We too can learn to praise and thank God for his goodness to us.

Checklist
- Prepare the prayer pod. As well as the children's craftwork, you may have a prayer cairn from the last session.
- An adult leader will need to keep an eye on any child who comes to use the pod.
- If using paints or glitter glue, have aprons or old shirts to protect children's clothes, especially school uniform!
- Remember to invite the parent/carers to join you twenty minutes before the end of the final session for coffee and cake round the craft campfire, and to see what the children have been getting up to.
- Note that there is not a DVD episode for this session.

7

World of a child
The importance of knowing we can trust God has run throughout *Target Challenge.* This is another story where David trusted God in a tough time. But we also need to know that being able to trust God is a cause for celebration at all times. Make sure there is plenty to celebrate in this session.

 **Hopscotch**
(up to 15 minutes)

See Session 2 for details.

NB: There is no 'Being still exercise' at this point. This activity has been moved to 'Hitting the Spot' in this session.

Finding focus

 **David as king**
(15–20 minutes)

There are dramatised Bible readings, which are 2 Samuel 5:1–4,17–20; 6:1–5 since there is no DVD episode. You'll need a space big enough to use as a stage, and the children who aren't acting in each scene will need to sit where they can see it.

What you need
- Two narrators and a director (could all be done by one person if necessary)
- Scripts for narrators and director (see page 74)
- A chair to represent a throne
- A bottle of olive oil
- Swords for the Philistines and one for David
- A letter for the messenger
- Something to represent a fortress (such as a play house from church toddler group)
- A big box to represent the Ark of the Covenant (sacred chest) and a skateboard or sledge as an ox cart to carry the chest on
- Musical instruments: shakers, tambourines, castanets (whatever you can get your hands on, including the ones used in Session 4).

What you do
Lay down the ground rules. Explain that the children are being actors, and actors always follow the director's directions. They may find all this very exciting, but it's important that they listen to the director and do what he or she says. Children who don't listen to the director will be asked to leave the stage and sit in the audience instead.

Split the children into three groups. Each group will practise and then enact one of the scenes on pages 74–75. The first narrator should read the introductions as animatedly as possible, and the second narrator should read the Bible passages slowly, with pauses at each stage direction so the children have time to follow

them. The director helps the children get into the right places with the right props at the right time (theoretically!).

> ❝ We broke up into three groups to prepare the scenes and we found some brilliant props to use. Involving the whole group in the final party was beautifully inclusive and a lovely way to end the drama. ❞
> *Vickie*

Hitting the spot

◎1 Being still exercise: Psalm 23
(10 minutes)

What you need
- A walking stick (shepherd's crook) and the sling from Session 1
- Some OHP/Powerpoint slides with images to illustrate Psalm 23 (optional: sheep/shepherd, fields, a stream, a dark valley, a feast)
- CD of instrumental music to play in background; CD player
- Rugs/mats

What you do
Introduce this by showing the children the shepherd's crook and sling and asking if they remember from Session 1 what sort of things a shepherd does (chases after sheep when they wander off; finds them if they're lost; protects them from wild animals). Explain that shepherds also move their sheep to different fields from time to time, where there's plenty of grass for them to eat, and water to drink. Say that when David wrote the psalm we're going to read today (Psalm 23), he was imagining God looking after him the same way as a shepherd looks after his sheep: protecting him, guiding him, feeding him. Now ask the children to find a space on the floor to lie on their backs with their eyes closed. Switch on the music and go through the usual routine of consciously tensing and relaxing different parts of the body. They might also concentrate on breathing, in and out, slowly a few times.

If you have slides for the children to look at, ask them to sit up again so they can see the screen (otherwise carry on with the meditation while they're lying down with eyes closed). Start the slide show and begin reading Psalm 23, slowly, with the added prompts for the children to think about. Pause briefly after each prompt:

7

Imagine you're a sheep (no baas, please!) with your shepherd always guiding you to the best fields of grass to eat, and the clearest streams of water to drink. If you wander off the path he comes to find you and bring you back to the flock.

> 'You, LORD, are my shepherd.
> I will never be in need.
> You let me rest in fields of green grass.
> You lead me to streams of peaceful water,
> and you refresh my life.
> You are true to your name,
> and you lead me along the right paths.'

Sometimes the path you have to follow might not be very nice – it could be rocky and difficult, or dark and creepy, and make you feel sad and worried. But you don't need to be scared because the shepherd is always with you and he's got his crook and his sling to protect you from wild animals.

> 'I may walk through valleys as dark as death,
> but I won't be afraid.
> You are with me,
> and your shepherd's rod makes me feel safe.'

Imagine a royal banquet like we had earlier with lots of lovely things to eat and drink – and God gives you the best seat and makes you feel really special. This is because he loves you.

> 'You treat me to a feast, while my enemies watch.
> You honour me as your guest,
> and you fill my cup until it overflows.
> Your kindness and love will always be with me each day of my life,
> and I will live for ever in your house, LORD.'

⑤ We'd found some lovely pictures to create a slide show for this meditation but it turned out we couldn't use them. The programme was corrupted. However, the children (and leaders) lay quietly and still all the way through and really entered into the psalm imaginatively. It was fascinating hearing them talk about their experiences afterwards. ⑤
Mary

 **Praise workshop**
(5–20 minutes)

What you need
- Paper
- Art and craft materials
- Magazines with relevant pictures
- Some copies of Psalm 23 for older children to look at

What you do
Explain to the children that, even after he became king, David kept writing songs and poems to praise God for being so great, and to thank him for all the good things he created. Ask the children to think about some things to praise God for. Children may either draw/paint/cut and stick pictures of things they want to praise God for (younger children), or write some down (older children). Older children might like to have a go at writing their own praise psalms. If stuck for ideas, look at Psalm 23 again.

◎₃ Role play
(5–20 minutes)

What you need
- Children who have enjoyed the drama and want to think of some real-life implications

What you do
Put the children in small groups and ask them to think of one situation when they have known God keeping them safe or treating them in a special way. This could be a time of danger or a pleasurable school trip to a beautiful or interesting place. How can they act this out for the rest of the group? How might they then express their thanks to God? If time allows, each group can show their drama to everyone else, explaining what they have done and why.

 **Learn and remember verse**
(5–15minutes)

What you need
- A large STOP sign
- Poster/OHP of Psalm 23:1 – 'You, LORD, are my shepherd. I will never be in need.'
- Small copies of the Learn and remember verse on page 69 for the children to take home
- Shepherd's crook and the sling from Session 1 for visual aids

7

What you do

Gather all the children in the prayer pod and show them the crook and sling again. They are going to learn the first verse of the psalm they heard during the 'Being still' exercise, so hopefully it will be easy to remember. Explain that it says that God will guide us like a shepherd and give us what we need to live. Repeat the Learn and remember verse several times, reading it to them once and then reading it all together. Don't forget to include the reference each time.

STOP can help us to pray.
Sorry (if we've done things to other people that are not kind and loving)

Thank you (that God keeps his promises, and his kindness and love is always with us – the children can use their own praise psalms here if they want to, or say thank you for the things they've included in their praise pictures)
Others (have they got a friend who especially needs to know God's love at the moment?)
Please (help me to trust you when things are going well – or not so well)
Amen!

Make sure that you say goodbye to each child individually and, if possible, talk with the person who has come to collect each child.

Some ideal programmes to use after Target Challenge:

So, Why God?

Steve Hutchinson

How do you introduce children to the Christian faith? Their questions are a good starting point! *So, Why God?* seeks to answer questions children ask about the Christian faith using the Bible and the stories of group leaders themselves.
A 12-week discipleship course for children aged 7 to 11.
£9.99 978 1 84427 222 8

High Five

Wendy Stanbury

Eight sessions for a midweek club or special event for children based on a Bible reading structure from Mark. Each session helps children explore how Jesus touched the lives of those around him. Additional activities encourage children to think about social justice issues around the world.
£9.99 978 1 84427 251 8

'You, LORD, are my shepherd. I will never be in need.'

Psalm 23:1

8

Session 8
David's king

Bible
Matthew 21:1–10

Aim
To show that God kept his promise to David that one of his descendants would always be king. Jesus was David's descendant, and the crowds in Jerusalem recognised him as a very special king, the Messiah, God's chosen one. But he was not like a normal, earthly king.

Checklist
- Prepare the prayer pod. As well as the children's pictures and crafts from each session, you may still have a prayer cairn, or you might want to build another one to show parents. Make sure there's plenty for parents to explore and discover in this area, when they arrive.
- If using paints or glitter glue, make sure you have aprons or old shirts to protect children's clothes, especially school uniform!
- There is not an episode of the DVD for this session.
- There is a lot to be fitted in to this session so keep an eye on the time!

Target practice

As this is the last session, you need to have plans for what you will do next for the children. Will you run another series or extend what you have done this term? Will you be able to do something more for family members? How might you integrate the children and their families into the wider church family? Make sure you communicate the options to those who have come to this final session and certainly include this in the take-home sheet if you are using them.

Make sure that you have extra adult help to befriend the parents and carers, ideally one of your church leaders as well.

Welcome the children to *Target Challenge*. Make sure everyone has either a name badge or a sticker and ensure anyone who has had a birthday is made to feel special.

⏱1 Dart ball
(up to 15 minutes)
See Session 1 for details. Today, when every child has had their go, gather them together to look at whose aim has improved the most over the eight weeks. (You could have two prizes, one for the biggest improvement and one for the highest score.)

⏱2 Penalty shoot-out
(up to 15 minutes)
NB This would clearly work best if you have an outside space

What you need
- Goalposts of some sort
- A football
- A spot marked to place the ball on each time
- An adult or older child in goal

What you do
Give each child a practice shot and then three goes to score a goal from the spot marked. Does anyone manage to score a goal, or even two or three? (If anyone gets three you probably didn'tput the best person in goal!!)

As this is the last session, you could play the children's favourite game at *Target Challenge* or the one that went best (which may or may not be the same!)

⏱3 Royal icing
(10 minutes)
What you need
- A table to work on
- Plain biscuits or un-iced fairy cakes (enough for two each – one for each child and one for the parent/carer who comes to meet them)
- Icing/writing icing/cake decorations/sprinkles
- A serving platter to display the iced cakes/biscuits when finished

What you do
Encourage each child to ice/decorate two biscuits or small cakes for the shepherds' campfire at the end of the session. When the iced cakes are done, display them on the serving platter to hand out when sitting round the campfire.
Note: Remember to make good use of supportive church members to provide home-baked plain fairy cakes and biscuits for icing.

⏱4 Prayer cairn
(5–10 minutes)

What you need
- Plenty of big pebbles

What you do
If there's a group of children who enjoyed building the 'God-with-us cairn' in Session 6, or some that missed that activity and might like to have a go, get them to build another cairn in

the prayer pod, reminding them of what cairns are for: to mark the path, or the top of the hill in wild places like mountains. Chat with the children about the fact that whenever David was worried about something, upset or afraid or not knowing what to do, he would ask God to help him and God always did. We can tell God about whatever's happening in our lives, and ask him to show us the way (like a cairn on a mountainside). When putting their final pebble on the pile of stones each child can pray, 'God is with us' or, 'Thank you God that you're with me when…'

5 Snack – shepherd's picnic
(5–15 minutes)

What you need
- Picnic rugs/blankets
- Cuddly toy lambs (optional)!
- Paper or plastic plates, cups
- Simple picnic: cheese or jam sandwiches and fruit or, if it's near a mealtime, a smaller snack. Remember to check for any food allergies.
- Drinks

What you do
Set the scene to create the mood of a picnic. Ask children to spread picnic rugs on the floor. Put the food in the middle of the 'table' so that they can help themselves to a couple of sandwiches, piece of fruit and a drink. Encourage adult helpers to chat with the children while you sit on the blankets and have your refreshments.

6 Being still exercise
(2–5 minutes)

What you need
- CD of instrumental music to play in background; CD player
* Rugs/mats

What you do
Ask the children to find a space on the floor to lie on their backs with their eyes closed. Switch on the music and go through the routine of consciously tensing and relaxing different parts of the body. They might also concentrate on breathing in and out slowly a few times. Read out the Learn and remember verses, one at a time, explaining that you will pause between each so they can think about what they mean. What else have they learned about God at

Target Challenge in the sessions they have been to? (*Best to keep this short.*)

Finding focus

1 David's king
(15 minutes)
No DVD this week

What you need
- The 'prophet' outfit from Session 2 (a cape and a staff)
- The children's coats
- A hobby horse

What you do
Dress a child as Zechariah the prophet. Tell them to try to look *incredibly* wise and *very, very* good! Then read the following introduction as animatedly as you can:
Do you remember seeing on the DVD (amend if necessary) how, when David was a young shepherd boy, Samuel the prophet, a messenger of God, came to visit the house of Farmer Jesse? He brought a message from God to say that Jesse's youngest son, David, was to be God's new king, even though David was the *last* person anyone expected God to choose! When David finally became king, God promised him, 'I will make sure that one of your descendants will always be king' (2 Samuel 7:16). So the Jewish people expected all their kings to be from the family of King David.

Well, hundreds of years later, long after Samuel and David had died, another prophet called Zechariah brought a message to the people of Israel to say that God was sending a very special new king to them, who would rule over all the earth. When this king arrived, he would ride into their capital city, Jerusalem, on a young donkey, a 'colt'. Zechariah said: (*An older child can read the next bit out, or ask a younger child to repeat it after you, phrase by phrase, in a loud voice*):
'Everyone in Jerusalem, celebrate and shout!
Your king has won a victory,
and he is coming to you.
He is humble and rides on a donkey;
he comes on the colt of a donkey.' (Zechariah 9:9)

Number the children from one to three, to divide them into three groups. Teach group 1 the shout, **'Hooray for the Son of David!'** (explaining that the people called God's special new king the 'Son of David' because they

World of a child
Jesus described himself as the Good Shepherd, so the final Learn and remember verse brings the themes of the whole series together. Only King Jesus can rescue his lost sheep and help us to find our way back to God. You may be able to point out the contrast of Jesus as an unusual king and as a shepherd.

Children who have been to *Champion's Challenge* will have focused upon the life of Jesus and there was a reference to Jesus' entry to Jerusalem in that programme in Session 4. You may wish to refer to that. Alternatively, you may have a number of children in the club who are familiar with the story of Jesus, although they may not have thought about him very often as a king. Encourage them to share their understanding.

8

expected him to be from King David's royal family).

Teach group 2, **'Blessed is the king who comes in the name of the Lord!'** (from Luke 19:38).

Teach group 3, **'Hooray for God in heaven above!'**

Ask the children to put their coats on and stand up, either side of a 'road' because they're going to pretend that they're the crowd in Jerusalem, trying to see God's special new king or Messiah riding into town on a donkey. Ask one child to be Jesus, riding on the hobby horse donkey towards the crowd, and then through the middle of it, over the coats. (Make sure the child who is playing the part of Jesus doesn't wear their shoes so the coats don't get dirty, but that they are careful not to slip!) Explain that one way the Jewish people welcomed a famous person was to spread clothes or tree branches in the road in front of them, like putting out a red carpet for a film star to walk on. They need to listen out for this moment in the Bible reading so they can put *their* coats on the floor in front of Jesus as he rides into town. They should be ready to give their shouts when you say, 'They were all shouting…' For the full crowd effect they keep shouting their words over and over again until you ask them to stop.

Read the Bible passage

Photocopy the Bible passage on page 75 and read aloud, emphasising the italicised phrases, pausing to give time for the actions.

Hitting the spot

Sit the children down. Some points to bring out when they are settled:

- Everyone in the city was excited when Jesus arrived on the back of a donkey because they knew it meant he was God's special king over the whole earth. (Children might have a variety of expectations of how royalty behave. You might want to explore that as a way to see what sort of a king Jesus was.)
- God had promised David that one of his descendants would always be king and Jesus really *was* a descendant of King David!
- Jesus' mum was called Mary and she was married to Joseph. As part of Joseph's family, Jesus could say that King David was his great-great-great-great (etc) grandfather!

At this point you can either do the 'Who is in your family?' exercise or simply show an example of a family tree to the children.

⊙1 Who is in your family?
(5–10 minutes)

What you need
- A4 piece of paper and something to write with

What you do

Ask each child to draw themselves and put their name on the bottom of the paper. Around themselves, they are to draw some of their relatives. For younger children this might be brothers or sisters or parents. But older children should be encouraged to draw more distant relatives. How many can they think of? Be aware that for some children this may be difficult or emotionally tough. As you do this, talk about families and generations that go back many years. Remind them that Jesus was a descendant of King David. His life and death was planned even before David was born! What does that tell them about God?

⊙2 Gathering up the sheep
(10 minutes)

What you need
- Strips of magnet
- Circles of card 5 cm in diameter
- Cotton wool
- Sticky black spots
- Glue
- A nail (not sharp), or something metal, tied to a piece of string that hangs from a stick at least 50 cm long

What you do

Ask the children to make as many sheep as they can, by sticking a blob of cotton wool on a circle of card, attaching a magnetic strip to the card and two black spots for eyes. Put all the 'sheep' in a closely marked-out area on the floor. Each child has 60 seconds to see how many sheep they can gather up/attract to the nail.

⊙3 Craft shepherds' campfire
(10 minutes for building fire, another 15–20 minutes with parents there)

What you need
- Some large stones (or big scrunched up bits of grey paper to look like stones)
- Dry logs/sticks or cardboard

- Art and craft materials including felt-tip pens, sellotape/Blu-tack and scissors
- Tissue paper (red, orange, yellow)
- A torch with good batteries
- Picnic rugs and blankets/shawls to sit on/wrap round people's shoulders
- Cuddly toy lambs for effect (optional)
- Hot chocolate in cups for children (made earlier and allowed to cool)
- Tea or coffee for adults
- Iced cakes or biscuits for all

NB You will need to sit around this campfire when parents join you, so build it with plenty of space around it.

What you do

Start off by placing the stones in a circle for a fireplace. If you have real logs/sticks, arrange them in a wigwam shape, leaving a gap in the middle for the torch. If not, colour some cardboard to look like wood and roll it up to make logs, then arrange it like a campfire, again with a space in the middle for the torch. Crumple up some large red pieces of tissue paper and tuck them into the heart of the 'fire'. Cut out flame shapes from the orange and yellow pieces of tissue paper and attach them to logs. Finally switch on the torch and put it in the middle of the fire for the full, glowing effect.

As the parents begin to arrive, create the mood of an open-air camp. Dim the lights so the campfire glow is the focus of attention. Encourage children to meet their parents/carers at the door and bring them in to sit round the 'fire' on the ground. Children may also want to put shawls, scarves or travel rugs round their shoulders as if sitting outside on a chilly evening. Serve hot chocolate for children, coffee for parents and iced cakes or biscuits for all and talk about what the children have enjoyed over the eight weeks of *Target Challenge* and what they've learned about King David and about God and prayer. Teach the children their final Learn and remember verse while the parent/carers are there.

 **Learn and remember verse**
(5–15 minutes)

What you need
- A large STOP sign
- Poster/OHP of John 10:11 – 'I am the good shepherd, and the good shepherd gives up his life for his sheep.'
- Small copies of the Learn and remember verse on page 69 for the children to take home

- Shepherd's crook and the sling from Session 1 for visual aids

What you do

Explain that this week's Learn and remember verse is something Jesus said about himself. 'I am the good shepherd, and the good shepherd gives up his life for his sheep.' We know that David risked his life when he fought bears and wolves to protect his sheep. David also risked his life for his country when he fought Goliath. Jesus, the Good Shepherd, sees us as his silly sheep, who've wandered off from God's ways and need rescuing. He gave up his life for us when he died on the cross so that we could find our way back to God, through him. Repeat the Learn and remember verse several times, reading it to them once and then reading it all together. Don't forget to include the reference each time.

You probably won't have time to use STOP this week, but if it seems appropriate, you *can* teach parent/carers the method! If you're using this week's material for an all-age service you will certainly want to include it.

Explain how STOP can help us to pray. This week we've been thinking about Jesus being the Good Shepherd who lays down his life for the sheep so we can pray:

Sorry (for when we've wandered from God's ways like silly sheep, and done things that hurt people)

Thank you (that Jesus is the Good Shepherd who gives up his life for his sheep)

Others (who haven't yet met the Good Shepherd)

Please (help me to remember that you love me even when I mess up, and will never leave me) Amen!

Make sure that you say goodbye to each child and, any accompanying carer, individually, and ensure that everyone knows about future plans for club members and their families.

8

'I am the good shepherd, and the good shepherd gives up his life for his sheep.'

John 10:11

Take-home sheet

Today's story (a summary):

Learn and remember verse:

Puzzle/something for the children to complete:

Requests for help/equipment:

Next session...

'Hide me in the shadow of your wings.'
Psalm 17:8

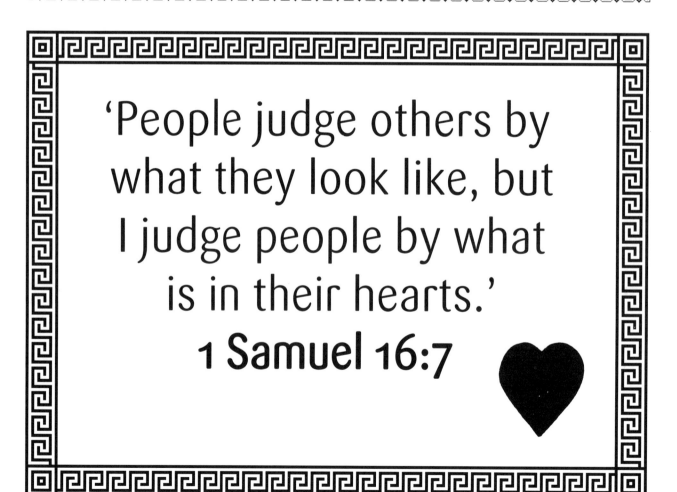

'People judge others by what they look like, but I judge people by what is in their hearts.'
1 Samuel 16:7

'I praise you, LORD, for answering my prayers. You are my strong shield, and I trust you completely.'

Psalm 28:6,7

'Shout praises to the LORD! Our God is kind, and it is right and good to sing praises to him.'

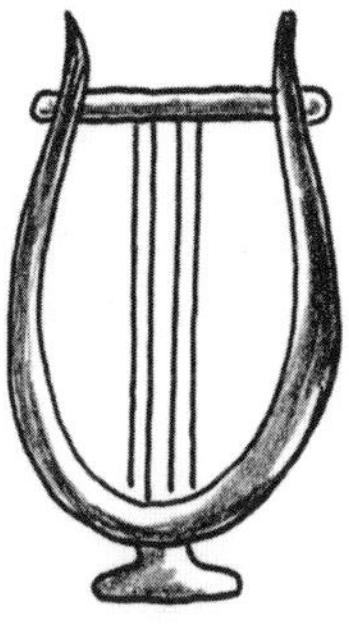

Psalm 147:1

'There is a friend who sticks closer than a brother.'

Proverbs 18:24

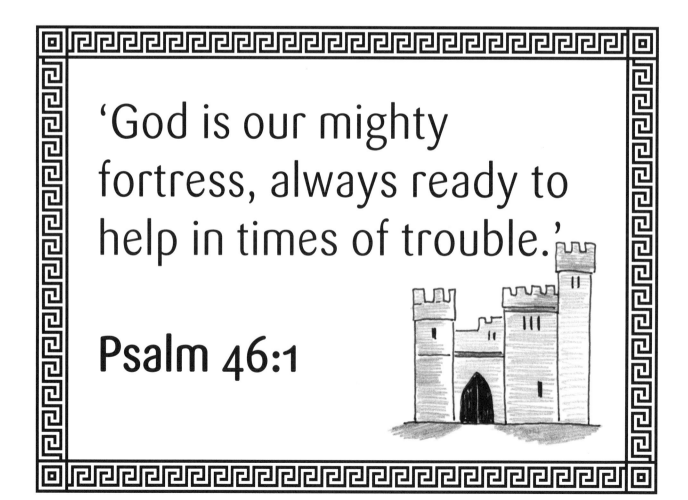

'God is our mighty fortress, always ready to help in times of trouble.'

Psalm 46:1

'You, LORD, are my shepherd. I will never be in need.'

Psalm 23:1

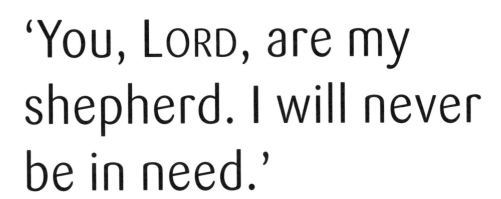

'I am the good shepherd, and the good shepherd gives up his life for his sheep.'

John 10:11

Session 1

1 Samuel 17:12–15; 16:19,21,23
David's father Jesse was an old man, who belonged to the Ephrathah clan and lived in **Bethlehem** in Judah. **Jesse had eight sons**: the oldest was Eliab, the next was Abinadab, and Shammah was the third. The three of them had gone off to fight in Saul's army.

   David was Jesse's youngest son. **He took care of his father's sheep**, and he went back and forth between Bethlehem and Saul's camp.
[King Saul sometimes felt troubled and frightened, and his royal advisers said he should find a musician to play soothing music. One of them had heard that Jesse's youngest son could **play the harp** well, and was also very brave so…]

   Saul sent a message to Jesse: "Tell your son David to leave your sheep and come here to me."
David went to Saul and started working for him. Saul liked him so much that he **put David in charge of carrying his weapons**.

   Whenever the evil spirit from God bothered Saul, David would play his harp. Saul would relax and feel better, and the evil spirit would go away.

Session 2

1 Samuel 16:1–13
One day [the LORD] said, "Samuel, I've rejected Saul, and I refuse to let him be king any longer. Stop feeling sad about him. Put some olive oil in a small container and go visit a man named Jesse, who lives in Bethlehem. I've chosen one of his sons to be my king." Samuel answered, "If I do that, Saul will find out and have me killed."

   "Take a **calf** with you," the LORD replied. "Tell everyone that you've come to offer it as a sacrifice to me, then invite Jesse to the sacrifice. When I show you which one of his sons I have chosen, pour the **olive oil** on his head." Samuel did what the LORD told him and went to Bethlehem. The town leaders went to meet him, but they were terribly afraid and asked, "Is this a friendly visit?"
"Yes, it is!" Samuel answered. "I've come to offer a sacrifice to the LORD. Get yourselves ready to take part in the sacrifice and come with me." Samuel also invited Jesse and his sons to come to the sacrifice, and he got them ready to take part. When Jesse and his sons arrived, Samuel noticed Jesse's oldest son, **Eliab**. "He has to be the one the LORD has chosen," Samuel said to himself.
But the LORD told him, "Samuel, don't think Eliab is the one just because he's tall and handsome. He isn't the one I've chosen. People judge others by what they look like, but **I judge people by what is in their hearts**."

   Jesse told his son Abinadab to go over to Samuel, but Samuel said, "No, the LORD hasn't chosen him."
Next, Jesse sent his son Shammah to him, and Samuel said, "The LORD hasn't chosen him either." Jesse had all seven of his sons go over to Samuel. Finally, Samuel said, "Jesse, the LORD hasn't chosen any of these young men. Do you have any more sons?"

   "Yes," Jesse answered. "My youngest son David is out taking care of the sheep."

   "Send for him!" Samuel said. "We won't start the ceremony until he gets here."

   Jesse sent for David. He was a healthy, good-looking boy with a sparkle in his eyes. As soon as David came, the LORD told Samuel, "He's the one! Get up and pour the olive oil on his head." Samuel poured the oil on David's head while his brothers watched. At that moment, the Spirit of the LORD took control of David and stayed with him from then on.

   Samuel returned home to Ramah.

Session 3

1 Samuel 17:4–11, 32–37, 40–51 (edited)

The Philistine army had a hero named Goliath who was from the town of Gath and was over nine feet tall. He wore a bronze **helmet** and had bronze armour to protect his chest and legs. He carried a bronze **sword** strapped on his back, and his **spear** was so big that the iron **spear**head alone weighed more than fifteen pounds. A soldier always walked in front of Goliath to carry his **shield**. Goliath went out and shouted to the army of Israel:

"Choose your best soldier to come out and fight me! If he can kill me, our people will be your slaves. But if I kill him, your people will be our slaves. Here and now I challenge Israel's whole army! Choose someone to fight me!"

Saul and his men heard what Goliath said, but they were so frightened of Goliath that they couldn't do a thing.

"Your Majesty," [David] said, "this Philistine shouldn't turn us into cowards. I'll go out and fight him myself!"

"You don't have a chance against him," Saul replied. "You're only a boy, and he's been a soldier all his life."

But David told him: "Your Majesty, I take care of my father's sheep. And when one of them is dragged off by a lion or a bear, I go after it and beat the wild animal until it lets the sheep go. Sir, I have killed lions and bears, and I can kill this worthless Philistine. He shouldn't have made fun of the army of the living God! The LORD has rescued me from the claws of lions and bears, and he will keep me safe from the hands of this Philistine."

"All right," Saul answered, "go ahead and fight him. And I hope the LORD will help you."

David picked up his shepherd's stick. He went out to a stream and picked up five smooth rocks and put them in his leather bag. Then with his sling in his hand, he went straight toward Goliath.

Goliath came toward David, walking behind the soldier who was carrying his **shield**. When Goliath saw that David was just a healthy, good-looking boy, he made fun of him. "Do you think I'm a dog?" Goliath asked. "Is that why you've come after me with a stick?" He cursed David in the name of the Philistine gods and shouted, "Come on! When I'm finished with you, I'll feed you to the birds and wild animals!"

David answered: "You've come out to fight me with a **sword** and a **spear** and a dagger. But I've come out to fight you in the name of the LORD All-Powerful. He is the God of Israel's army, and you have insulted him too! Today the LORD will help me defeat you. Then the whole world will know that Israel has a real God. Everybody here will see that the LORD doesn't need **swords** or **spears** to save his people. The LORD always wins his battles, and he will help us defeat you."

When Goliath started forward, David ran toward him. He put a rock in his sling and swung the sling around by its straps. When he let go of one strap, the rock flew out and hit Goliath on the forehead. It cracked his skull, and he fell facedown on the ground. David defeated Goliath with a sling and a rock. He killed him without even using a **sword**. When the Philistines saw what had happened to their hero, they started running away.

Session 4

1 Samuel 18:6–16
1. David had killed Goliath, the battle was over, and the Israelite army set out for home. As the army went along, women came out of each Israelite town to welcome King Saul. They were singing happy songs and dancing to the music of **tambourines and harps**. They sang:
2. Saul has killed a thousand enemies; David has killed ten thousand enemies! (Could you put this to music or ask the children to compose a tune?)
3. This song made Saul very angry, and he thought, "They are saying that David has killed ten times more enemies than I ever did. Next they will want to make him king." Saul never again trusted David.
4. The next day the LORD let an evil spirit take control of Saul, and he began acting like a crazy man inside his house. David came to play the **harp** for Saul as usual, but this time Saul had a spear in his hand. Saul thought, "I'll pin David to the wall." He threw the spear at David twice, but David dodged and got away both times.
5. Saul was afraid of David, because the LORD was helping David and was no longer helping him. Saul put David in charge of a thousand soldiers and sent him out to fight. The LORD helped David, and he and his soldiers always won their battles. This made Saul even more afraid of David. But everyone else in Judah and Israel was loyal to David, because he led the army in battle.

Session 6

1 Samuel 24:1–11,16–20
When Saul got back from fighting off the Philistines, he heard that David was in the desert around En-Gedi. Saul led **three thousand** of Israel's best soldiers out to look for David and his men near Wild Goat Rocks at En-Gedi. There were some sheep pens along the side of the road, and one of them was built around the entrance to a cave. Saul went into the cave to relieve himself.

David and his men were hiding **at the back of the cave**. They whispered to David, "The LORD told you he was going to let you defeat your enemies and do whatever you want with them. This must be the day the LORD was talking about."

David sneaked over and cut off **a small piece of Saul's robe**, but Saul didn't notice a thing. Afterwards, David was sorry that he had even done that, and he told his men, "Stop talking foolishly. We're not going to attack Saul. He's my king, and I pray that the LORD will keep me from doing anything to harm his chosen king." Saul left the cave and started down the road. Soon, David also got up and left the cave. "Your Majesty!" he shouted from a distance.

Saul turned around to look. **David bowed down very low and said: "Your Majesty, why do you listen to people who say that I'm trying to harm you? You can see for yourself that the LORD gave me the chance to catch you in the cave today. Some of my men wanted to kill you, but I wouldn't let them do it. I told them, 'I will not harm the LORD's chosen king!'** Your Majesty, look at what I'm holding. You can see that it's a piece of your robe. If I could cut off a piece of your robe, I could have killed you. But I let you live, and that should prove I'm not trying to harm you or to rebel. I haven't done anything to you, and yet you keep trying to ambush and kill me."

"David, my son – is that you?" Saul asked. Then he started crying and said: "**David, you're a better person than I am**. You treated me with kindness, even though I've been cruel to you. You've told me how you were kind enough not to kill me when the LORD gave you the chance. If you really were my enemy, you wouldn't have let me leave here alive. I pray that the LORD will give you a big reward for what you did today. **I realise now that you will be the next king, and a powerful king at that.**"

Session 5

1 Samuel 20:1–3, 12,13, 17–23,35–42
[Scene 1: At the palace]

Narrator: David escaped from Prophets Village. Then he ran to see Jonathan and asked,
David: "Why does your father Saul want to kill me? What have I done wrong?"
Jonathan: "My father can't be trying to kill you! He never does anything without telling me about it. Why would he hide this from me? It can't be true!"
David: "Jonathan, I swear it's true! But your father knows how much you like me, and he didn't want to break your heart. That's why he didn't tell you. I swear by the living LORD and by your own life that I'm only one step ahead of death."
Jonathan: "I swear by the LORD God of Israel, that two days from now I'll know what my father is planning. Of course I'll let you know if he's friendly toward you. But if he wants to harm you, I promise to tell you and help you escape. And I ask the LORD to punish me severely if I don't keep my promise."
Narrator: Jonathan thought as much of David as he did of himself, so he asked David to promise once more that he would be a loyal friend. After this Jonathan said:
Jonathan: "Tomorrow is the New Moon Festival, and people will wonder where you are, because your place will be empty. By the day after tomorrow, everyone will think you've been gone a long time. Then go to the place where you hid before and stay beside Going-Away Rock. I'll shoot three arrows at a target off to the side of the rock, and send my servant to find the arrows. You'll know if it's safe to come out by what I tell him. If it is safe, I swear by the living LORD that I'll say, 'The arrows are on this side of you! Pick them up!' But if it isn't safe, I'll say to the boy, 'The arrows are farther away!' This will mean that the LORD wants you to leave, and you must go. But he will always watch us to make sure that we keep the promise we made to each other.

[Scene 2: In a field]
Narrator: In the morning, Jonathan went out to the field to meet David. He took a servant boy along and told him,
Jonathan: "When I shoot the arrows, you run and find them for me."
Narrator: The boy started running, and Jonathan shot an arrow so that it would go beyond him. When the boy got near the place where the arrow had landed, Jonathan shouted,
Jonathan: "Isn't the arrow on past you? Hurry up! Don't stop!"
Narrator: The boy picked up the arrows and brought them back to Jonathan, but he had no idea about what was going on. Only Jonathan and David knew. Jonathan gave his weapons to the boy and told him,
Jonathan: "Take these back into town."
Narrator: After the boy had gone, David got up from beside the mound and bowed very low three times. Then he and Jonathan kissed each other [goodbye] and cried, but David cried louder. Jonathan said,
Jonathan: "Take care of yourself. And remember, we each have asked the LORD to watch and make sure that we and our descendants keep our promise forever."
Narrator: David left and Jonathan went back to town.

Session 7

2 Samuel 5:1–4,17–20; 6:1–5

Scene 1 [Props: throne and olive oil]
Narrators 1 & 2, Israel's leaders, David, Chief leader

Narrator 1: After Saul and three of his sons were killed in a big battle with the Philistines, David did eventually become king, just as God had promised when the prophet Samuel came to visit Jesse's farm. It turned out that being a hard-working shepherd boy was good practice for being a good king.
Narrator 2: [*David sitting on his throne, centre-stage*] Israel's leaders met with David at Hebron [*Leaders come on stage and bow down before David, then stand up*]…
…and said, "We are your relatives. Even when Saul was king, you led our nation in battle. And the LORD promised that someday you would rule Israel and take care of us like a shepherd."
During the meeting, David made an agreement with the leaders [*David shakes hands with each of them*] and asked the LORD to be their witness. [*They all kneel down with hands together and eyes closed, praying*] Then the leaders poured olive oil on David's head to show that he was now the king of Israel. [*Probably best if Chief Leader <u>pretends</u> to pour the olive oil on David's head!*]
David was 30 years old when he became king, and he ruled for 40 years… [*David sits back down on throne and leaders leave the stage*].

Scene 2 [Props: swords, letter and fortress]
Narrators 1 & 2, the Philistines, David, a messenger
Note: Choose a sensible child to play David. He's going to have to win a sword fight later!

Narrator 1: The Philistines were still Israel's enemies (remember the giant, Goliath, who David killed with a pebble) and the Philistines didn't like the idea of David being Israel's king. In fact they wanted to get rid of him. But whenever David was in danger, he knew where to turn…
Narrator 2: [*David sitting on his throne, centre-stage*] The Philistines heard that David was now king of Israel, and they came into the hill country to try to capture him. [*Philistines come on stage, brandishing swords and looking threatening*]
But David found out and went into his fortress. [*Messenger brings David a note, and David runs to his fortress and goes inside*]
So the Philistines camped in Rephaim Valley. [*Philistines mime putting up tents!*]
David asked the LORD, "Should I attack the Philistines? Will you let me win?" [*David kneels down with hands together and eyes closed, praying*]
The LORD told David, "Attack! I will let you win."
David attacked the Philistines and defeated them. [*Make sure the children stage a battle without really hurting anyone! The Philistines have to all end up lying on the floor, so David's won*]
Then he said, "I watched theLORD break through my enemies like a mighty flood." So he named the place "The Lord Broke Through." [*David sits back down on throne*]

Scene 3 [Props: sacred chest, 'ox cart' and musical instruments]
Narrators 1 & 2, 30,000 soldiers (or at least two!), David, people of Israel – children from all groups can join in for this bit

Narrator 1: David knew that his success was down to God. One of the first things he did as king was to bring an important piece of temple furniture back to the capital of Israel, Jerusalem, and have a big party in praise of God. The sacred chest had angels with wings, and a throne carved on it. It reminded the people that God had protected them for centuries and that he was their <u>real</u> King, more powerful than any king on earth.
Narrator 2: David brought together 30,000 of Israel's best soldiers and led them to Baalah in Judah… [*David leads the soldiers marching in a line onto the far side of the stage, where the sacred chest is. The soldier at the back of the line pulls the 'ox cart' after him*]

They were going there to get the sacred chest and bring it back to Jerusalem. *[Two of the soldiers lift the chest very carefully and put it on the 'ox cart']*
The throne of the LORD All-Powerful is above the winged creatures on top of this chest, and he is worshipped there. They put the sacred chest on a new ox cart and started bringing it down the hill from Abinadab's house… *[The two soldiers with the chest and cart lead the way back across the stage slowly, pulling it after them, with David and the other soldiers following]*
Some of the people of Israel were playing music on small harps and other stringed instruments, and on tambourines, castanets, and cymbals. *[Everyone on stage, with musical instruments, for a noisy, joyful crowd scene]*
David and the others were happy, and they danced for the LORD with all their might. *[Let everyone dance for a while and then ask them to stand in a line and take a bow while all the leaders clap. After this the director should ask them to sit down on the rugs again]*
Narrator 1: David still enjoyed music and praising God more than anything else. We know this because lots of his songs, called psalms, are included in the Bible. They were used for worship in the temple that his son, Solomon, built. The psalms are still used by Christians in worship today. This week we're going to hear the whole of one of David's psalms; the one we mentioned last week that says, 'The Lord's my shepherd…'

Session 8

Matthew 21:1–10 (edited)
When Jesus and his disciples came near Jerusalem, he sent two of them on ahead. He told them, "Go into the next village, where you will at once find a donkey and her colt. Untie the two donkeys and bring them to me. If anyone asks why you are doing that, just say, 'The Lord needs them.' Right away he will let you have the donkeys." So God's promise came true, just as the prophet had said, "Announce to the people of Jerusalem: 'Your king is coming to you! He is humble and rides on a donkey. He comes on the colt of a donkey.'"

The disciples left and did what Jesus had told them to do. They brought the donkey and its colt and laid some clothes on their backs. *Then Jesus got on.* Many people *spread clothes in the road*, while others put down branches which they had cut from trees. Some people walked ahead of Jesus and others followed behind. *They were all shouting,* "Hooray for the Son of David! God bless the one who comes in the name of the Lord. Hooray for God in heaven above!"

When Jesus came to Jerusalem, everyone in the city was excited and asked, "Who can this be?"

Elastic band harp for Session 4

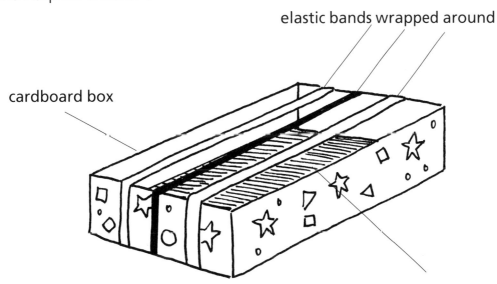

cardboard box

elastic bands wrapped around

stickers to decorate

Badge templates for session 1

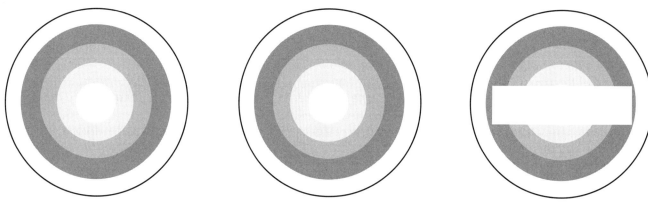

Target practice scoresheets for session 1

Target practice scoresheet	
Name:	Score
Session 1	
Session 2	
Session 3	
Session 4	
Session 5	
Session 6	
Session 7	
Session 8	

Picture frame for Session 2

glue here

glue here

glue here

Stick the frame to a piece of card the same size as the frame.

Outline of Goliath for Session 3

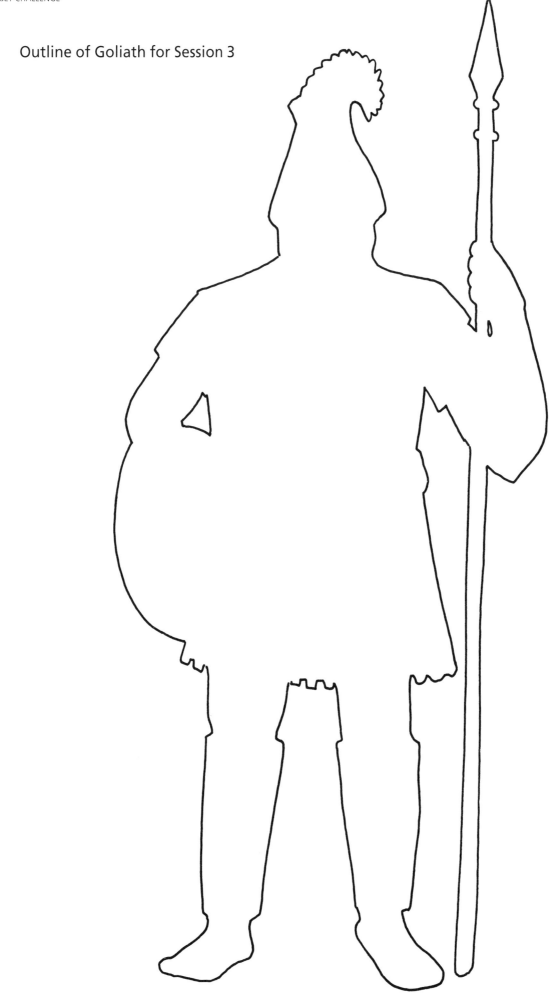

Other resources

The Strong Tower
Robert Harrison and Roger Langton

Ten retold stories about children in the Bible who faced tough times! These stories are beautifully illustrated and movingly explore how these ten children and young people coped with their pressures of life. For example, what was it like for Gershom, the son of Moses, when his dad was criticised by God's people, as they prepared to cross the Red Sea? Or what about Paul's nephew who visited his uncle in prison? Great stories to read to a whole group of children in your club.

£7.99 978 1 84427 122 1

Into the Bible – 101 routes to explore

101 extracts from the Bible to tell God's BIG story and help children find their own way through the Bible, with navigation tools to ensure they don't get lost. A brilliant resource to equip you in your club to help children handle the Bible text (from the CEV) without them becoming overwhelmed by the sheer extent of the Bible as a big book! All the key stories and passages are included in this child-friendly book.

£8.99 978 1 84427 295 2 (also available as multiple copies)

(A CD of 24 RE lesson outlines using *Into the Bible* for use in the Primary classroom is also available. For more details visit www.scripturenion.org.uk/intothebible)

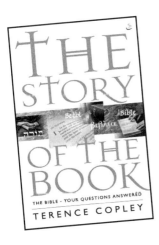

The Story of the Book
Terence Copley

Find out more about the Bible: Who wrote it? How was it put together? What is its future? These difficult questions and many more are answered in a down-to-earth style in this 'unstuffy' book about God's Word – essential reading as you use the Bible in your club.

£8.99 978 1 84427 131 3

eye level clubs...

- are for boys and girls aged 5 to 11.
- are for children who are not yet part of a church (as well as those who are).
- don't assume that children know much about Jesus or have had any experience of church.
- recognise that all children are open to God and the wonder of his world, and that all children can have valid spiritual experiences, regardless of church background.
- aim to give children one of the best hours in their week.
- provide opportunities for appropriate and respectful relationships between children and adults, working in small groups.
- plan to introduce children to the Bible in ways that allow for imagination, exploration and learning difficulties.
- are led by those who long to see children become lifelong followers of Jesus Christ.
- are led by those who will put themselves at a child's level, so that together they can catch sight of Jesus.